ALSO BY MARK YAKICH

A Meaning for Wife

The Importance of Peeling Potatoes in Ukraine

The Making of Collateral Beauty

Unrelated Individuals Forming a Group Waiting to Cross

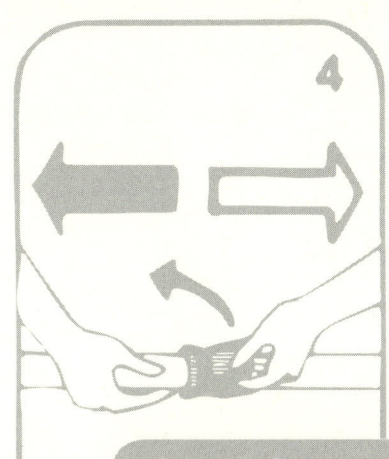

CHECKING OUT
MARK YAKICH

Copyright © 2011 by Christopher Schaberg & Mark Yakich.
All rights reserved.

533 Webster St.
New Orleans, LA 70118

Acknowledgements
For publication of excerpts of this book, thank you to *Brevity*, *The Millions*, *Narrative Magazine*, *The New York Times*, and *Propeller Magazine*.

For advice and financial support, thank you to the English Department of Loyola University, to Mary McCay, and to John Synder of the Center for Music and Arts Entrepreneurship. This book is sponsored, in part, through the Center's "The Year of the Writer" initiative.

For design, collaboration, and dear friendship, thank you to Nancy.

For time, inspiration, and love, thank you to Lara and Annie.

ISBN: 978-0-615-46640-8
Design & layout by Nancy Bernardo.
Printed by Thomson-Shore in Dexter, Michigan.

For more airport & airplane stories, visit: airplanereading.org

CHECKING OUT
Mark Yakich

I LIKE TO SIT IN my car and watch them. Sometimes I don't even need the binoculars to see their beauty marks: burn scars behind rear-mounted engines or scuffs and dings thoroughly pocking the bottom of fuselages. Right now, for instance, the one before me is at least twenty-five years old, carries more than 5000 gallons of fuel, and waits there interminably, number one for take-off. It's really a piece of shit as compared to the newer models. But knowing that a piece of shit can fly, I feel a strange empathy.

I imagine sitting on that American Airlines MD-80: alternating between looking down at the book in my lap and staring back out at the airport and highway through the porthole window, comprehending neither the words of the book nor how the hulking machine will get off the ground. A line from Rilke comes to me—*Beauty is nothing but the beginning of a terror*—and my hands start to sweat despite the ice-cold AC. I take a drink and then another. Although I believe differently each time I fill the flask at home, the bourbon does nothing for me now.

Alcohol, drugs, sex, TV, exercise, gaming, shopping, gardening, napping, a six-pack of low-fat double-dutch chocolate pudding—there are any number of ways to get through the day. The only thing that keeps me going, however, is a regular drive out to the New Orleans airport. I sit in my car in the cell

 CHECKING OUT

phone lot, witness the last of the planes take-off and land, and get worked up into a neurotic, though life-affirming, frenzy.

This is the problem: I can remember a time when I truly enjoyed flying, but it seems impossible to get back there, and the more I fly, the farther away that time seems.

MY FIRST FLIGHT WAS IN 1975 when I was five years old: Boston to Chicago before a cross-country family move. There are no photos of the event (somehow I expect there to be) yet I have held on to a memory of blue, orange, and white striped seats—to which I ascribe the notion that the plane must have belonged to United Airlines. I also have the vague impression that I climbed a spiral staircase, which would have made the plane a 747, an aircraft that weighs almost a million pounds on take-off, one-third being fuel and less than one-tenth being passengers and cargo, and that is composed of six million parts, half of which are fasteners and rivets. But after doing some research, it seems unlikely that a 747 would have been used on such a short domestic route.

I didn't fly again until I was 19 and a sophomore in college: Chicago to Florida for spring break. A high school friend's parents paid for my ticket because I said I didn't have the money, which was a lie: I just didn't want to fly. I'd never been south of Champaign-Urbana before, so stepping out of the airport in Sarasota I felt that the thick, humid air was as invigorating and exotic as the flight.

After my first overseas flight at age twenty-one, I memorized the date, place, flight number, and scenario of every major plane crash since 1903 because I thought the knowledge would help ease a growing apprehension. But I didn't yet realize that, like consciousness, too much information can be paralyzing.

My fear has grown over the years, but I never recognized it as more than a personal inconvenience until I met the woman who would become my wife. A month into our relationship, I was supposed to fly to Chicago to visit my parents for a family reunion. The trouble was we lived in Berkeley. This was summer 2003, so not only was I terrified of flying (I hadn't in two years) but I also feared a nuclear explosion in the Bay Area, as I had scrupulously followed all newspaper reports speculating that a dirty bomb could be sent undetected to a U.S. port city in a cargo container. I went to bed each night listening to the San Francisco Bay winds skirt the windows, with our calico cat safely perched on my chest, mumbling last-minute mantras

 CHECKING OUT

before checking to make sure my iodine tablets were still safe in the drawer of the nightstand. Sometimes I took them from the drawer and put them in the pocket of my flannel pajamas, thinking that I might not be able to get to the nightstand in time in case of a blast.

But flying frightened me more than a dirty bomb. And so when I told my wife-to-be I was taking BART to Oakland's airport to go visit my parents, I was actually walking two miles down to the Amtrak station in Berkeley to catch a Chicago-bound train. The ride took more than 48 hours, and I have never told anyone about this lie until now.

3

AS A CHILD GROWING UP in 1970s Chicago, I would get up early on Sunday mornings to pick up the *Chicago Tribune* from the driveway. Not because I really enjoyed the comics, but because I wanted to read the "Tomorrow" section of the paper, which was filled with articles about the future. The one I recall best detailed how thousands of people would live on moon colonies by the year 2000. I remember showing my mother the article and telling her that when the time came for volunteers, I would gladly step forward. When she asked why, I said because everything on Earth had already been discovered.

I have never asked my father if he is afraid to fly. In fact, there are many things I've never asked him that I should before he dies. He worked on the Apollo that went to the moon, the F-15 fighter plane, and the Patriot Missile. We've talked about these things in general terms, but never in specifics. When I was sixteen it was revealed to me (it had been a secret for about ten years) that he'd been diagnosed with schizophrenia. I'd always known that he was extremely intelligent—he was an electronic engineer at Raytheon and then Northrop. His title was "specialist," which my mother told me meant that they had him work on engineering problems that other engineers had spent months trying to figure out—he would come up with a solution in a matter of days. But he was very introverted and didn't talk much about this work, and not because the work was classified.

None of this matters much, I suppose, to my ongoing fear of flying. And because I was adopted, what does it matter if he were afraid to fly? It's not like I could claim "my genes made me do it." At least not his genes.

Citing air sickness and prohibitive expense, my mother hasn't been on a plane in 35 years. In that same time,

 CHECKING OUT

my father has flown a couple of times for business. The last time he flew was in the early 1990s for an engineering consultant job. From a pay phone in Atlanta he called my mother and said, "You were almost a widow." Then he proceeded to tell her how the plane, which he just disembarked, had made a quick landing after take-off because a part needed to be changed. He didn't relish the thought of getting back on the same plane, but said that he would see her soon at O'Hare in Chicago. Before hanging up he added, "If I don't make it, the notebooks with the secret Jesus codes are in the basement freezer." This was the first indication to my mother that he may have had a schizophrenic relapse.

The first time I flew out of the country it wasn't exactly to escape my family; I was in college and had already gotten far enough away. During the plane ride, I don't recall being very afraid. I was probably too excited about what I would experience in Vienna as a study abroad student. I remember flying into Frankfurt on a 747. I was sitting next to a FedEx pilot who pointed out that we'd been circling the airport for twenty minutes. I mumbled an uh-huh, but he sounded worried. I said that a friend of mine had recently received his license to fly a Cessna and said that a plane can just glide in if it runs out of fuel. "Not this one," the pilot said, "if we run out of gas, this thing will float like a brick doesn't." It was at that moment, I believe, that I first began to recognize that I had an existential problem with flight. Only years later would I figure out that that pilot had stolen the line about the brick from *The Hitchhiker's Guide to the Galaxy*.

BECAUSE I DON'T FEEL COMFORTABLE telling people about my fear of flying, I call it "checking out"—as in *I got on the plane and just checked out*. But "checking out" refers to twin experiences: the wonderfully strange, zoned-out feeling of actual flying, especially when I'm looking out the plane's window down on the great expanse of Earth, and the persistent thought that the plane is going to crash and I'll soon be checking out with the rest of the passengers in a firey ball of metal and plastic.

If I had to quantify this second checking out on a scale of 1 to 10, with 1 being not at all afraid and 10 being very afraid, I would rate myself an 8. Nine would seem melodramatic, but anything less would be a lie. Sure, at times after a couple of connections and a couple of drinks, my fear hovers around 5. But then there are those moments as the plane speeds down the runway during take-off or dodges storm clouds that my fear

 CHECKING OUT

escalates to a little excrement in the underwear, a panic attack, a 9. To reach a 10, I suppose, the plane would actually have to crash.

Here is one of many items I don't understand about plane crashes: After a crash or incident, transcripts for the cockpit chatter are released to the public in censored form. The censorship isn't for material that might incriminate or embarrass crew members, but for expletives. All expletives—shit, fuck, damn—are substituted with #. For example, below are the last words of the pilots of American Eagle Flight 4184. The plane had been flying over northwest Indiana, waiting to land at Chicago's O'Hare Airport, when it suddenly fell from the sky.

> **1557: 16.3 HOT- 1** Are we out of the hold?
>
> **1557: 17.3 HOT- 2** Uh, no, we're just goin' to eight thousand.
>
> **1557: 19.4 HOT- 1** OK.
>
> **1557: 20.0 HOT- 2** And uh, ten more minutes she said...
>
> **1557: 22.1 CAM-** [Sound of repeating beeps similar to overspeed warning starts and continues for 4.6 seconds]
>
> **1557: 23.3 HOT- 2** Oop.
>
> **1557: 24.7 CTR** Kiwi Air seventeen, descend and maintain six thousand.
>
> **1557: 26.2 HOT- 1** We, I knew we'd do that.

1557: 27.4 HOT- 2 I's trying to keep it at one eighty.

1557: 28.2 KW17 Kiwi Air seventeen, eleven point five for six.

1557: 29.2 HOT- 2 [Ramping repetitive thud sound]

1557: 28.9 HOT- B [Wailing sound for 1.2 seconds similar to "whooler" pitch trim movement]

1557: 29.9 HOT- 1 Oh.

1557: 31.2 HOT- B [Wailing sound for 1.7 seconds similar to "whooler" pitch trim movement]

1557: 32.8 HOT- 2 Oops, #.

1557: 33.0 CAM- [Sound of three thumps followed by rattling]

1557: 33.5 CAM- [Sound of three sets of repetitive rapid triple chirps similar to auto-pilot disconnect warning lasting 1.09 seconds]

1557: 33.8 HOT- 2 #.

1557: 35.2 CAM- [Single horn similar to altitude alert signal]

1557: 35.6 CTR Kiwi Air seventeen, direct Chicago Heights, direct Midway.

1557: 36.9 HOT- ? OK

1557: 37.0 HOT- B [Intermittent heavy irregular breathing starts and continues to end of recording]

 CHECKING OUT

1557: 39.0 KW17 Direct the Heights direct Midway, Kiwi Air seventeen.

1557: 38.8 [Repetitive thumping sound heard on first officers channel]

1557: 39.9 HOT- ? Oh #.

1557: 42.4 HOT- 1 OK.

1557: 43.7 CAM- [Single horn similar to altitude alert signal]

1557: 44.0 CAM- [Sound of "growl" starts and continues to impact]

1557: 44.2 HOT- 1 All right man...

1557: 45.8 HOT- 1 OK, mellow it out.

1557: 45.8 CAM- [Sound of repeating beeps similar to overspeed warning starts and continues to impact]

1557: 46.7 HOT- 2 OK.

1557: 47.1 HOT- 1 Mellow it out.

1557: 47.7 HOT- 2 OK.

1557: 48.1 HOT- 1 Auto- pilot's disengaged.

1557: 49.4 HOT- 2 OK.

1557: 52.8 HOT- 1 Nice and easy.

1557: 54.9 CAM- 5 Terrain, whoop whoop.

1557: 56.6 HOT- 2 Aw ##.

1557: 56.7 CAM- [Loud crunching sound]

1557: 57.1 END OF RECORDING

For me, expletives have their place in our language and that place is one I visit with some regularity. In an argument, there's nothing that cuts to the bone quite as nicely as a well-used "fuck," "shit," or "dickhead." But that is not the reason I chose the above excerpt from the cockpit voice recorder of American Eagle Flight 4184. I chose this flight because I was on its counterpart, if you will: the American Eagle commuter flight traveling the same route but in the opposite direction, Chicago to Indianapolis.

I remember the evening distinctly, because it was Halloween 1994 and I was traveling with my girlfriend, who would later become my fiancée for twenty-three days and then persona non grata thereafter. We were flying back from a weekend trip to Washington D.C. to visit a college friend of mine who was in graduate school for creative writing at George Mason University.

My friend's guest bedroom was painted a pale lavender that matched the curtains and the bedspread on which my girlfriend and I made love three-and-a-half times in two days leaving a stain that I couldn't remove with citrus shower gel. None of these details is relevant except that the plane crash has cemented them into my head.

Even if this sister plane had not crashed, I would have remembered this particular model of plane. The ATR-72 is a twin-turboprop, and this was the first time I flew in a plane that

 CHECKING OUT

did not have jet engines: I remember closely checking out the propellers while walking across the tarmac to board (passengers board and exit from the rear while cargo goes in and out the front).

The flight from D.C. to Chicago was uneventful, and the Chicago to Indianapolis leg wasn't particularly rough, just filled with ominous clouds off to one side and at times that opaque gray that often envelops a plane in inclement weather. We landed, climbed down from the back of the plane, walked the tarmac, and arrived in a lounge area of the Indianapolis airport. Immediately we noticed a small crowd looking up at a small TV screen.

A commuter plane, carrying 68 people, had crashed in a soybean field near Roselawn, a small town upstate. I would later read that the plane plowed into the earth so hard (430 mph) that it virtually disintegrated (except for a part of the tailwing where the AA insignia could still be read). The coroner wrote that the passengers died of "multiple anatomical separations secondary to velocity impact of aircraft accident."

The Federal Aviation Administration determined the cause of the crash to be a "ridge of ice [that] accreted beyond the deice boots while the airplane was in a holding pattern." But weather wasn't apparently the only guilty party. Relatives of 16 victims brought a case against the FAA when it was discovered that the ATR-72, a French-made craft, was known to be susceptible to ice build-up. It soon became a clichéd American-Franco battle, one side blaming the other for inadequate oversight and response. Before the case went to trial, though, the defendants agreed to a record $110 million settlement and an apology in open court.

On further investigation, officials concluded that there was essentially nothing they could do to remedy the heavy icing that can occur on the ATR-72's wings. The deicing boots could not be extended far enough to prevent other possible crashes. But there were hundreds of new or relatively new ATR-72 crafts throughout the world—what to do? Airlines came up with a simple solution: Stop flying the plane in temperate climes. Today, for example, American Airlines regularly uses the plane in the Caribbean.

Every once in a while I think about the Roselawn crash. Sometimes around Halloween, sometimes when I fly a regional jet, sometimes when I use citrus shower gel. And somewhere around the date of the crash is, in fact, when I first began keeping a journal and writing poems. They were awful, middle school-style love poems, and over the next three years I began to love writing them more than anything else, including the women to whom the poems were written. At the time of this discovery, I was living in Brussels, Belgium, where I enjoyed a comfortable, if modest, expatriate life. My obsession with poems would not abate, and finally I came back to the States so that

 CHECKING OUT

I could begin graduate school in creative writing at Louisiana State University.

I will never forget my first trip to Baton Rouge: The final connecting flight from Houston was on a Continental Airlines ATR-72. Disembarking from the back of the plane, I stepped onto the tarmac and welcomed the full-oven heat of late-July Louisiana.

TODAY, I AM A POET. But as a child I found Dr. Seuss's books irritating, and I only checked books out of the library because I liked how they decorated my nightstand. In grade and middle school, the only thing I remember reading or writing were love letters, carefully folded in triangles like the flags of remote countries I couldn't name. And looking back, I believe I only wrote and read those letters because they seemed to be required of my middle class upbringing.

The first poem I remember hating was Matthew Arnold's "Dover Beach," on which I had to write a report in 10th grade. My English teacher's name was Mrs. Vrba. She had a broken foot for most of the year, and I had once arm-wrestled (ever so adroitly) her daughter Tricia in 7th grade. Tricia and I were at the State Science Fair at the University of Illinois at Champaign-Urbana. I took first place with a zoology project about how horseshoe magnets affected earthworms (my mother's idea; Mother also typed and wrote most of the report; I was proficient at the design and stenciling of the peg board; Father did the sawing and the screwing); but more importantly I took Tricia's hands in mine in the indoor/outdoor pool at the Howard Johnson's one dimly-lit afternoon. I hope Tricia, too, can still recall how we detained each other in that lukewarm bath, my hands glossing her violet-and-white-striped one-piece. Telling myself this story of Tricia during her mother's poetry lessons was the only way I saw poetry as relevant: that is, poetry served only as a distraction from real life.

When I went to college, I didn't fly. My father shuttled me the three-hour drive. And I still disliked poems. In fact, I took only one English class, and I majored in political science. Instead of love letters, there was now cunnilingus. I enjoyed it much more than writing, and my love interests probably did as well. Before I was 25, I had read three novels, of which two were *The Catcher in the Rye*. That's not a boast; rather, it's something I'm ashamed of—like my fear of flying. But when I was 25 I moved to Belgium on a research grant and began living in a one-room lean-to attached to a 14th-

 CHECKING OUT

century building in the small college town of Leuven where everyone around me spoke Flemish. In other words, I was isolated and had no friends. I soon realized, however, that books and the voices in them made for decent companionship. And because most poems are brief, I could make a lot of friends fast.

For years I wouldn't admit to being a poet, and for even more years I wouldn't admit to being an aerophobe. Both seem unfit for modern life. Now, I am also a professor of creative writing. I teach poetry for a living, which, to me, is at once a silly and vital occupation. The poet Marianne Moore once called poetry contemptible and genuine in the same breath, which is not the same thing as calling it genuinely contemptible. For the same reason poetry is irrelevant as compared to, say, heart surgery or fire fighting or trash collecting, it is also important. Because poetry can't make money, it escapes commodification (most of the time). Its irrelevance becomes its importance. I don't know how exactly poetry is pertinent to a fear of flying. I just know that the two often link up in my head, as in this poem by A.R. Ammons:

Small Song

The reeds give
way to the
wind and give
the wind away

These four lines were the first lines of poetry I ever enjoyed. I could and could not make out what they were telling me. These seven words (a few repeated) couldn't have been any simpler and yet they made (and still make) my mind do little backflips. As in W.B. Yeats's famous line *How can we know the dancer from the dance?*, I still keep trying to discern which is which: Are the reeds only reedy because they're moved by the wind, or is the wind only windy because we detect its effects? It is, of course, not necessary to decide between the two. But no matter how many times I read these lines, I feel ridiculously compelled to pick one over the other—as if I've just survived a water landing and must choose between my wife or our son, only one of whom I can save.

TO ME, THE COCKPIT HAS always been inscrutable: Two seats enveloped by an impossible number of lights, buttons, switches, toggles, and joysticks. In fall 2009, however, this inscrutability was raised to a new level. A Northwest flight overshot its runway by 150 miles. Luckily the plane was still in the air—so it made a large U-turn over Wisconsin

 CHECKING OUT

and landed safely at its destination, the Minneapolis airport.

Industry analysts and laypeople alike speculated that the pilots had fallen asleep at the helm, especially after it was reported that they'd been sent all kinds of electronic and radio messages from air traffic controllers to no avail. It did not go unreported, as well, that military fighter jets were at the ready in case the errant plane decided to hit something large and vulnerable in Wisconsin, such as a moose—no matter there are no longer moose in Wisconsin to my knowledge. A few days after the incident, the pilots' excuse for the lapse was that they had been on their laptop computers working on some kind of new airline scheduling program. In other words, they were still working, just not on the most pressing tasks at hand. Because the cockpit voice recorder only records for half an hour before looping over itself, and the pilots were out of communication for more than an hour, investigators suggested that it was going to be very difficult to determine whether the pilots were telling the truth.

Immediately, however, it occurred to me that someone should really check these pilots' cocks for chafing or burns. From my extensive experience of working and sitting in a car, I know there is no way to work on a laptop in such a cramped space as a cockpit without incurring serious heat and, most assuredly, wounds to the area of the genitalia. One may try to place something like a hardback book between the laptop and one's cock, but it had better be a rather thick hardback book, for heat more than a few minutes will penetrate anything thinner, including magazines or, I imagine, flight plans. There is therefore no way these two men could have had laptops on their respective laps without injuring themselves. The only other possibility is that the pilots did something to cool down this tender area, but it is not for me to speculate further.

The only thing worse than overshooting the runway is never reaching it—or having to find a poor substitute. Captain Sully of the "Miracle on the Hudson" fame (January 2009) wasn't the first, and likely won't be the last, to successfully water-ditch a commercial aircraft.

In the history of water-landings, in fact, Sully is superceded by whoever piloted Pan Am Flight 943, Clipper Sovereign of the Skies, on October 16, 1956. En route from Hawaii to San Francisco, this plane lost the use of two of its four engines in the middle of the night and at an altitude of 21,000 feet. The pilots calculated that they couldn't make it back to Honolulu or push on to California. Fortunately, there was a U.S. Coast Guard cutter, which was serving as an ocean station between Hawaii and California, within a half-hour's flying. After emergency preparations, hours of circling, and a dry run at landing, the plane ditched around 8 a.m. near the ship. All crew and passengers

 CHECKING OUT

were saved, but the plane and 44 cases of live canaries in its cargo hold sunk to the bottom of the ocean. What is perhaps most amazing is that the entire ditching and rescue was captured on film by the U.S. Coast Guard and is now available on YouTube.

From the airplane ditching in the Hudson River, we remember Captain Sully. But what about Sully's copilot—doesn't he deserve some credit? Almost no one can name him; two heroes are simply not as interesting as one. A seminal example: Charles Lindbergh was not the first man to fly across the Atlantic. Surprised? He was the sixty-seventh. But he was the first to fly it solo—such is the notoriety we grant being alone. Push the idea of heroism being singular a bit further: Christianity, Judaism, Islam, and other religions insist that there cannot be multiple gods, but only one god (monotheism). And technology, the modern-day religion and hope for many, is no different. In parlance, it's "a cure" for cancer, not "cures" for cancer.

And yet here is Lindbergh in an interview shortly before his death: "I realized that if I had to choose, I would rather have birds than airplanes." I am not the first to point it out, but I probably point it out more than most: An airplane overhead looks more like a flying cross than it looks like a bird. Jesus wasn't the only one crucified that day, but He's the only one we remember.

WHETHER IN WATER OR ON land, here is what passengers look like before a plane crashes:

On the one hand, they appear comfortable—as if they are relaxed or meditating. On the other hand, they look tight-necked, blissed-out, preparing for impact, ready to meet their maker....

Yet now that I examine these dummies more closely, why aren't they hunched over in crash position? And how come no one is holding that baby! This photo is from a test plane (a Boeing 720 set for retirement after 20,000 flight hours) that was

 CHECKING OUT

crashed in the Mohave Desert on December 1, 1984. Through the FAA, the Secretary of Transportation sponsored the test which was to determine, among other things, energy-absorbing seat designs and improved cabin fire safety. The plane was flown by remote control, and anti-misting kerosene (as jet fuel) was used to prevent any post-crash fire. But the crash landing didn't go as planned. The engine on the left wing hit the ground first, the plane yawed, and a fireball erupted inside the cabin. Despite the fact that firefighters took about two hours to put the fire out, the FAA estimated that about 19 of the 53 passengers might have survived. There is no information as to whether or not the baby lived or died.

DESPITE BEING OVER-SCHOOLED, OFTEN HAVING to take a job in an unwelcoming small town, worrying for years over possible tenure, and being compensated by the white-collar equivalent of a ditch-digger's salary, a professor is a lucky son of a bitch. I don't know whether "academic freedom" truly exists any longer at colleges, but freedom from spousal oversight still does. In other words, my wife doesn't question when I drive out here to the airport—because I don't tell her. I mean, I tell her that I'm going to go work on my book, but she assumes I'm at my office or at the library on campus. And a professor's "research" can take him anywhere, so if I'm not at one of those two places it's no problem. I have my cell phone; I have my cell phone lot.

If part of my research involves watching movies in the car on my laptop, well, so be it. These days, it's impossible to watch a movie at home. Since our son was born my wife and I have seen exactly three movies. (What parent at the end of the day can make it through an hour-and-a-half or two-hour movie without nodding off?) And because my wife and I are always too brain-dead to read before bed, we have found watching an episode of a TV series—at a mere 45 minutes—an indispensable nightly ritual. Our son is now three years old, which means we've run through numerous series—from *Six Feet Under* to *The Forsyte Saga* to *Columbo*.

Our latest fascination is with *Mad Men*. I'm not that interested in ad men or in scenes of early 1960s New York City, but the dialogue is so sharp and smart that I wasn't surprised when the first episode of the second season featured the main character reading, and later reciting, from the poet Frank O'Hara's collection *Meditations in an Emergency*. Frank O'Hara is not only the right poet for the job (he wrote quintessential "city" poems); he is also the first poet I was obsessed with. But it's not O'Hara's city poems that interest me as much as his love poems, which, by turns, play sentimentalism off banality and surrealism off realism. I would even go so far as to argue that O'Hara is the greatest love poet of the twentieth century—though most poetry readers know him almost exclusively for his "I do this, I do that" poems, often thought of as simple, random lists written while walking the streets of Manhattan.

Mad Men is anything but simple. In the second episode of the second season, the precipitating event is a plane crash. And not just any plane crash. American Airlines Flight 1 took off from Idlewild Airport (today's JFK) on March 1, 1962, in clear skies. Two minutes later the plane nose-dived into Jamaica Bay. None of the 95 passengers and crew survived. In the *Mad Men* episode, two of the ad bosses walk into the agency that morning to find all their employees in a massive football-style huddle. It is an eerie moment for the viewer, not only because everyone is huddled up (around what turns out to be a radio), but because everyone is taking the news as if a loved one had been on the plane. Or maybe, it is more important that they are huddled around one media device, not football-style but campfire-style. On the entire floor of a Manhattan ad agency, that little boxy radio was their only link to outside news; it is a quaint sight considering even the most mundane office floor today, with each desktop a lively stream of headlines, status updates, and news bits.

As a plane crash, American Airlines Flight 1 isn't very

interesting. As an example of the reporting around a plane crash, it's fascinating. "Tragedy in Jamaica Bay" reads a headline of the March 9, 1962 issue of *Time* magazine. "It was ideal flying weather" is the first line. The same day "American One" (as the doomed plane is called) crashed, John Glenn was given a ticker tape parade in New York City for being the first American to orbit the earth. Here is a passage from the article describing the wreckage of the plane:

> A minute after the crash, it lay like a giant, shattered fish just beneath the transparent waters of the bay, with scattered debris and flakes of aluminum skin glinting on the tufts of marshland. The only signs of life were clouds of wheeling sea gulls, roused from a nearby bird sanctuary, and a dozen helicopters that whirled to the scene like a swarm of dragonflies.

If I were teaching this excerpt in a poetry class, I would draw my students' attention to the sheer amount of figurative language. The airplane is described as a giant, shattered fish—converted from a plane into a fish, but also turned enormous, and then solidified into something that could be shattered. Scale and material have been warped: in crashing, the plane has left the figurative ground. The fishi-

 CHECKING OUT

ness continues with "flakes of aluminum skin glinting on the tufts of marshland"—we are in a phantasmagorical nether region, between land and sea, fallen from the air. The imagery becomes even stranger: disturbed sea gulls become "wheeling" clouds (to mix metaphors atmospheric and machinic), and helicopters become "a swarm of dragonflies"—the plane crash has landed us humans in a world where categories of the human and non-human collapse, and everything is subject to dramatic revision. With reporting like this, who needs poetry?

What is naive about this *Time* article is the tone of near disbelief: Who would have thought that a new, cutting-edge aircraft could—*gasp*—crash! The innocence both soothes and piques my interest, until the article arrives at a familiar trope that I thought only got bastardized in the late 1990s: irony.

> Ironically, 17 passengers had transferred to
> American One at the last moment, when
> a United Air Lines flight was canceled.

What exactly is "ironic" about a flight being canceled and passengers being rerouted? This happens every day, and its meaning is never intended to be taken as its opposite. Nearly avoided crashes do not constitute irony any more than crashes consummated. When we sense an intriguing or inexplicable coincidence we often call it "ironic," when we really want to say "what an intriguing and inexplicable coincidence." It is this same impetus, I believe, that is behind what my college religion professor termed "God of the gaps." Whenever a certain phenomenon or event can't be explained or accounted for, people often attribute it to God until at some point it is demystified. (The tricky thing about getting rid of God is that it's like trying to throw away a garbage can: you need a bigger garbage can to do it.)

The article closes by stating that the crash "may keep its secrets hidden forever in the muck of Jamaica Bay." Perhaps at some point in the future someone will stumble upon one of those secrets: of its 25,000 acres of marshland, the bay is losing about 40 acres per year. In the end, the *Time* article about the crash seems more distant than the crash itself. The article foregrounds the fact that there were multiple millionaires on the flight—is that, finally, what made the crash a "tragedy"?

Now here I am at the end of the *Mad Men* episode—my wife in the bathroom brushing her teeth and our toddler fast asleep in our bed—turning on the computer. I've done my research on American Airlines Flight 1, and now it's time to check eBay again—I've been watching dozens of auctions for weeks now, trying to find a good deal on a Fisher-Price airplane from the late 1960s or early 1970s. Three weeks later I will get a box in the mail with a plastic airplane made in 1980 (it won't be

 CHECKING OUT

as nice as the earlier models but it'll be far less expensive). And I will have to teach our son not to kick the plane against the wall, but to zoom it on the floor and then up in the air around the room and back down for a soft landing. But no matter how many lessons I give, he will prefer to use the plane in the bathtub, and he will teach me that better than the vintage Fisher-Price houseboat, which I spent too much money on a month ago, the plane will float.

AS COMPARED TO RIDING IN an automobile, Wilbur Wright called flying "real poetry." This appears especially true looking down at puff-pastry clouds from a porthole window, sitting completely still yet traveling more than five hundred miles an hour, warm and safe and sipping a cocktail in relative anonymity.

That said, I have experienced a similar poetry by simply sitting in my car at the airport—particularly when I close my eyes and try to meditate. This goes back to the summer of 2006, when a fellow poet and friend invited me to attend a ten-day vipassana retreat (what I later would call "meditation camp"), outside of Rockford, Illinois. He asked, and I immediately said yes. I knew my days of bachelor-type adventuring were winding down: my wife and I were preparing to have kids. Knowing only what my father had told me about his meditation experiences, which involve a new age religious movement called The Summit Lighthouse, "ascended masters," UFOs, battles between light and darkness, and the mystical "voices" he has tuned in over the years, I decided that I'd see what meditation might reveal to me. The most attractive feature about vipassana, however, was its potential use in relieving my anxiety during flight.

Its adherents claim that vipassana meditation is what Buddha practiced, and even if that isn't true vipassana certainly seems like the "purest" version of meditation I can think of. Vipassana is devoid of mantras, visualizations, spiritual beings, or any other accoutrement, and is defined as "observing things as they actually are, not just as they *appear* to be." You simply sit in whatever position you like, say, lotus position, indian-style, or legs tucked under knees, close your eyes, and, well, sit. Sounds straightforward, but the trouble comes when your mind won't follow your body; the mind doesn't like to sit still. The other small element (at least at camp) is that you aren't allowed to talk (even to yourself) or communicate with anyone in any way (no making eye contact at meal time or during group sits).

When you meditate, you sit with eyes closed and ob-

 CHECKING OUT

serve. But you "observe" only what your body tells you. If you have a pain, for example, you are simply to notice the feeling, not to wish it away or power through it. It's a kind of "this too shall pass" attitude, which you're also supposed to employ when you have a "good" feeling (e.g. warm tingling or sensual rush). This is a kind of bio-feedback practice, except that you're not supposed to adjust mind or body to any changes.

The purpose of the camp is to teach you the technique by doing it, so that you can then apply it in your daily life. If, for instance, someone gets angry at you, raises his voice, and spits vitriol, your tendency is to defend yourself by immediately getting angry. This is natural—no reason to beat yourself up about it. But were you instead to observe your body's reaction (increased heart rate, flushed hands, tightened neck) to his initial anger, you might be able to change your behavior—and even if you couldn't change your behavior, simply noting what is happening to your body might be enough to temper it.

It sounds simplistic, and it is, which is also most likely the reason vipassana is damn near impossible to do. Fellow campers dropped out (including my "roommate" with whom I shared a bathroom), often in the middle of the night, knocking on the instructor's dorm room, getting their car keys and sneaking off into the darkness for the highway and civilization.

Keeping silent wasn't that much of a problem for me. Much harder, however, was sticking to the rule against masturbating—another no-no, of course—and I broke it only four or five times in the shower.

After spending the first three days of camp detoxing my mind of all its recent memories of home and work, I settled into the daily routine: 4:30 am, rise and meditate in your room; 6:00 am, meditate with the group; 8:00 am, eat breakfast; 9 am, meditate in your room; 11:00 am, meditate with group; 1:00 pm, eat lunch; 2 pm, meditate in your room; etc. Bedtime was at 10:30 pm.

When I meditated (eyes closed, of course) I would visualize each part of my body, systematically observing from head to toe. This was incredibly difficult to do without focusing on the unpleasant sensations that usually occurred in my back. If the pain was extreme, the only thing that would take my mind off of it was picturing myself having sex with my wife. Five seconds into that picture and the pain magically disappeared. At some point, I realized that this must work because all the blood was going to my groin and not to my brain or back. Otherwise, I have no recollection of what I actually thought about while meditating those ten days.

Each evening there was a brief respite from medita-

 CHECKING OUT

tion. As a group we watched a video of the master teacher S.N. Goenka; this felt to me like a prime time TV show you look forward to. Goenka gave interesting lectures, often employing anecdotes, illustrations, and humorous parables to impart the wisdom of vipassana. I can't recall any of his stories exactly, but I do remember his mentioning Cumaean Sibyl, a Greek prophetess who wrote answers to life's questions on oak leaves that quickly blew away and were lost. That lesson had to do with the impermanence of everything, and how the self doesn't really exist but in an impermanent state. In Goenka's words—now that I look them up—"nothing is a final product; everything is involved in the process of becoming." Re-reading that now, it sounds like a lot of hippie shit. But at the time, while meditating all day long, those words—perhaps any words—pleased my ear. From Goenka's mouth, again, "Liberation [from misery] can be gained only by practice, never by mere discussion." So in a way, those evening TV lectures were only pep-talks, not metaphysical answers.

By lights-out time I was tired enough to sleep, and each night I dreamed violent dreams that one by one systematically featured a member of my immediate family. I woke every morning to my own stifled gasps and moans and a sweat-drenched pillow.

The entire meditation camp experience is difficult to convey. It's part voluntary prison sentence, part self-denial, and part enlightenment. Three parts that can't be separated by the end of the experience, as in trying to get the egg or flour or baking powder back out of the sliced cake. And it certainly isn't as badly poetic as that metaphor. If there is a metaphor for the experience of meditating, I am certain that any self-respecting meditator would reject it outright.

When the retreat ended, I drove the six-hour trip home in silence. Not once did I feel the need for talk radio or music. My mind felt different, less anxious and more self-aware of its container. There was a slowness to my movements, or rather a consciousness to them I'd never had before.

When I got home, my wife was waiting for me, along with her sister and our niece who were visiting us from NYC. The first thing I wanted to do was make love to my wife, so we snuck off to the bathroom. The second thing I wanted to do was sleep; the ten days of meditation had worn me out. Our niece, however, had other plans. As the three adults were preparing dinner, she decided the sofa would make a fine trampoline. After we heard the screams, we ran into the family room to find blood all over her blouse, face, and long blond hair. She'd cut her head on the glass coffee table. My sister-in-law was hysterical, and I nearly slapped her à la the movies.

 CHECKING OUT

I'm not sure if meditation had prepared me for an emergency, but I was extremely calm in that moment. I quickly got my sister-in-law and niece to the car and even seat-belted them in. I raced to the hospital speedily but not wildly. Within the hour, my niece was stitched up and giggling at the photos of her red-orange hair I'd taken in the emergency room's waiting area.

I thought I'd done pretty well in this first stress test, and I hoped it would carry over to a flight I was set to take the following week. As we taxied onto the runaway at Detroit's airport, I began to feel the well-known, but always fresh, hell of my anxiety. Although I wasn't in the half-lotus position I had used at camp, I tried to observe what was happening to my body. Sweaty palms: check. Palpitating heart: check. Hyper-sensitive hearing for bangs, thuds, and crunching: check, check, check. And then I felt my breathing become shallower, my neck relax, and my feet feel lighter. It wasn't the vipassana-style observation that was easing my body, however; I'd experienced this phenomenon before: it was my body and mind preparing to let go, preparing to die.

ONE TIME, READY TO FLY from Chicago to Brussels, I was absolutely certain that the plane I was about to get on would explode. In the pre-boarding area of O'Hare Airport, I couldn't help but notice a very large man clad in a long, black leather coat. I was sitting a row over in a position where I could see him but he couldn't see me very well. He looked decidedly glum at one moment and then irritated the next. I don't know if I was actually suspicious of his being a terrorist or person-of-interest or whatever it is we call dubious-looking characters now, but he certainly gave the appearance of a man who was concealing something.

Over the years of flying I had noticed other such dodgy-looking passengers (almost always men) and let it go. But sitting there at the departure gate, I couldn't take my eyes off this particular man. I felt I had to do something, to tell someone something, and just as I was going to approach an airline worker at the counter, I chided myself for being a paranoid idiot. When my section of the plane was announced to board, I waited for him to make a move first. I walked a few people behind him as we funneled into the jetway, but his seat was further back than mine, so I lost sight of him once we were on the plane.

It is difficult to describe how responsible (or guilty) I felt because I had a strong intuition that this man was dangerous. I kept thinking, what if he blows up the plane and

 CHECKING OUT

I didn't do anything? Is that more cowardly than being embarrassed by notifying the authorities? I compromised: I wouldn't tattletale on him now, but I would watch him the entire flight. With permission from a flight attendant, I took an empty seat two rows back and across the aisle from my subject. It was difficult to keep my gaze on him constantly, and I felt a migraine coming on, but after I began imagining making love to the attractive woman seated next to him, I was fine.

Two hours into the flight, as attendants were serving a second round of beverages, he rose from his seat with a pained countenance. Still wearing his full-length leather mantel buttoned to the top, he walked past my row to the back of the plane. I began to sweat. This was it—he was going to ignite himself, or take out some plastic explosives, or at the least open the emergency hatch at the back of the plane. I made a move to get up and follow him, and then I sat back down. I berated myself for judging this man based on a black coat, beady eyes, and my outlandish sense of doom. I focused my attention on the attractive brunette, and put down my tray table so that no one would notice my erection.

About ten minutes later, the man lurched back into his seat. Now something was odd. I detected it in the faint gust of wind he made as he settled in: cigarettes. The bastard had been smoking in the lavatory! Before I had a chance to get too worried about a sizzling butt in the trash receptacle, a flight attendant raced past me toward the cockpit. Two other attendants came from the opposite direction, partially blocking my view. They questioned him; he shook his head, calm for once. The two attendants turned and proceeded back up the aisle to the front of the plane.

I wondered how come no one was double-checking the lavatory. It was an old plane; I'd have wagered that those smoke detectors weren't working anyway. I waited, relieved and yet still anxious to see what would happen. After a few minutes there was more activity. At first I thought it was another flight attendant, but then I realized it was the first officer or the captain standing in the aisle of the man's row. The man was shaking his head again, but this time he looked uncertain. The pilot was jotting down a note. He then tore off a slip of paper and handed it to the man. The man said something and then laughed. Passengers around the man began whispering and word spread throughout the cabin: The pilot had written him a $10,000 fine for smoking.

Thinking back on it now, the problem I have with this story is neither the ludicrous fine nor my extreme paranoia—the problem is whether or not I believe this is *my* story. If I recall correctly, a friend related the nugget of this tale to me when I first told him about my fear of flying. Since that moment, I've told this story so many times as if it were my own, picturing all

of its scenes and details (I can tell you, for example, the socks I was wearing—dress socks, one dark blue and one black)—that this story has become more mine than my friend's. And who knows—maybe my friend made it up or heard it from someone else. For it is only a *story*, made of words; whoever's actual experience it was is long gone, the fine paid or forgotten. And now that I've told you this story, it is—like so many airplane stories—partly yours as well, true and not true, a myth that you can believe in.

WHEN I WAS TWENTY-FIVE I experienced a crisis of faith, of sorts. Even though I had been raised both a Catholic (dad) and a Protestant (mom), I knew deep down that the stories of the Bible were just that—stories. But I also felt a need to test my disbelief. While I was living as an ex-pat in Belgium, I decided to take an extended vacation one holiday to the Middle East. My main aim was to walk from Jerusalem to Bethlehem on Christmas Eve. During take-off on a plane out of Brussels headed for Tel Aviv I felt relaxed, as I was seated between an orthodox rabbi and an Islamic cleric. *What was God going to do*, I thought, *take down two holies?* But then I realized perhaps their holy powers might cancel each other out if the plane went down.

After a month in the holy lands, I was set to come back home to Brussels. Security at Ben Gurion Airport in Tel Aviv was incredibly organized and incredibly insane. When I made my journey in 1996, long before governmental terrorism alerts of "orange" or "elevated," the airlines warned you to arrive three hours before your flight out of Ben Gurion. I had to get a ride the night before, eight hours ahead of schedule, and what I remember most about spending the night in the airport were the trash cans.

I was sitting on a suitably uncomfortable lounge seat, trying to sleep upright, but all I could do was watch a man visit each of the five or six trash cans in the area, sticking his head into each one. At first I thought he had perhaps lost something. But after the fourth or fifth round, I realized that he was an un-uniformed security officer checking the trashcans for explosives.

When I finally began my walk through security, I was soon aware that I was being singled out. In those days, the word "profiling" hadn't yet entered the vernacular (at least in America). Traveling alone as a young male with a Middle Eastern complexion (I'm half Lebanese) helped by a week-old beard—never mind the U.S. passport—made me a potential hazard. At least that's what I told myself.

At the first checkpoint, they asked me where I had

 CHECKING OUT

been (Jaffe, Jerusalem, Bethlehem, Amman, Petra), why (to have fun?), with whom I had stayed (hostels only), and finally where my map was. "Map?"

"Yes, show us your route, what you visited, where you walked, your trail." I dug around the mess of my backpack, which reeked of the kilo of cardamom-infused coffee I was lugging back home, finally locating my *Let's Go Israel!* Inside, I found my map where I had made scribbles with women's names I'd tried to sleep with along the way. It wasn't embarrassing until a condom and a nude photo of a young Spanish-Irish woman I was semi-dating back in Brussels popped out of the book (the condom had been taped to the back of the photo in an effort to keep me disease-free, if not monogamous).

The security people didn't crack a smile. When it was over I was exhausted. But then I was shuffled off to a second checkpoint where a hot, uniformed, young Israeli woman, obviously doing her military service, asked me the same questions. When they started in at the third checkpoint, I almost laughed aloud at the absurdity of it all but stopped myself for fear of a fourth checkpoint; I was beginning to doubt my own journey's narrative, especially after I stumbled on a few events when they made me recite it backwards.

When I finally got on the plane back to Brussels, I

should have felt relief. Relief that the hassle of security was over; relief that the plane was safer now that all its passengers had been intensely scrutinized and screened; relief that I was going home. But I felt none of it. I felt more anxious and more vulnerable than ever before about flying. And something more had been jarred loose in me. I began asking myself what all my narratives meant or added up to, and thinking about who I really was—how at once I was and wasn't Lebanese. And then the significant question came: How would my life have been different had I been born in Beirut, and not in Boston? Looking back now, I still come up with the same answer: I can't say who I might have become under only slightly skewed circumstances. Or what I might have been carrying instead of coffee in my backpack on that day, on that plane.

I TELL MY BEN GURION Airport story to a close friend who used to work for United Airlines, and he tells me a story about his brother's toothpaste smuggling. Apparently, his brother likes to smuggle a special kind of organic toothpaste (5.5-ounce tube) through security checkpoints. He simply places the tube

 CHECKING OUT

in his back pocket before passing through the metal detector, and because the tube is plastic, it does not set off the alarm. He passes through security every time with his illegal toothpaste. This man also happens to be a pilot and a certified flight instructor. My friend wonders whether his brother's toothpaste smuggling might lead to other nefarious acts, and therefore whether he should report him to Homeland Security and suggest that he be placed on the No Fly List. I have met my friend's brother and while he is a little eccentric, he is also a nice guy who once helped me move into the house I now live in. He single-handedly carried a loveseat up three floors of stairs without a nick to the walls. But that is not why I am thinking of this man now. I am wondering if the best way to get rid of my fear of flying is too simple. I am wondering if I should get out of the car, walk into the airport, get in the security line, and scream *Bomb, bomb, bomb!* until the authorities inscribe me into their special list forever.

AS THE POET WORDSWORTH SAYS, "The child is the father of the man." Maybe he's right—I have to be like a child again in order to re-appreciate flying—but there's only one man who has ever made me feel comfortable about the experience. Although I've never seen him in person and I frankly don't understand what the big deal is about *The Big Lebowski*, I am obsessed with Jeff Bridges' performance in the movie *Fearless*.

Most likely I saw the movie when it first came out in 1993 and thought it was a decent drama. But watching the movie more than 15 years later, with a seriously heightened fear of flying (I'd only flown three times before 1993), I was stunned. (If you've never seen the film, you might want to stop reading here. If you are curious, you can watch the film's trailer on YouTube; it's a trailer that doesn't tell the whole movie in miniature or give away the ending as nearly all trailers do today.)

The movie, in a nutshell, is the story of what happens to Max Klein (Jeff Bridges) after he survives a plane crash. One of the main plot lines is that Max, who says the crash was the best thing ever to happen to him, tries to help another survivor (Rosie Perez) whose 18-month-old son died in the disaster. The film's crash is modeled after the real-life DC-10 that lost all hydraulics one summer afternoon in 1989 an hour into its flight, stayed aloft for another 45 minutes, and then crash-landed at the airport in Sioux City, Iowa.

Max's flashbacks to moments of the harrowing crash punctuate the plot, until the end of the movie when we see the

 CHECKING OUT

final minutes before impact. Here, the camera focuses on Max, who we know to be a fearful flyer, as he's writhing in anguish. Inter-cut are flashes of action in the cabin—in particular, passengers handing over all their sharp objects, including jewelry, high heels, pens, and even eyeglasses, to a flight attendant who throws them into the lavatory and slams the door. Then, something—a piercing light, sun reflecting off of the plane's wing—catches Max's eye. His face lights up, and his gaze is fixed for a distended moment. The look of terror on his face slowly morphs into a look of peace. He turns from the light and the window and leans his head back; we see him from above, his face has gone from peaceful to blissful—not unlike the look on plane crash test dummies (see page 21).

"This is it," Max says in voiceover, "this is the moment of your death...I am not afraid, I have no fear." He takes the hand of his best friend and business partner who's seated next to him, and tells him it's going to be okay. Then, he spots a boy sitting all alone at the front of the plane. He squeezes his best friend's hand and leaves his seat to go comfort the boy.

To the jaded viewer (and I must admit I am often one), all of this seems like sheer heartstring plucking. And maybe it is—but it's done fucking beautifully. One of my mantras to my students is that if you're going to write a poem it'd better do something that no other form of media can do. I ask the question: If you're going to attempt a narrative or depict a scene in a poem, what are you going to do that can't be done in a novel, for example, or better in a movie? Then, I give them the example of reading a poem about someone dying—the deathbed scene, usually at a hospital—how this kind of poem almost never moves me, but an episode of *ER* or *House* will bring me to the verge of tears every time. Why is that? I ask and then answer: Because the medium of video moves me much more—that impact of the image and word over the word alone.

As I write this now, I realize that I have failed to abide by my own lesson: on many levels, *Fearless* moves me more than my own writing about my fear of flying. At the end of the movie, the director Peter Weir combines three things that prompt pathos: imminent fear of a crash, vulnerability of a child, and haunting music. And it's the third that really drives home the tragedy: Henryk Gorecki's Symphony No. 3, Op. 36 plays the length of the final sequence and on into the credits. This is particularly eerie to me: without knowing about this final scene, I have turned to this same piece of music, again and again, for years, blasting it through my headphones while flying through rough turbulence.

One movie reviewer calls this final sequence "a truly

 CHECKING OUT

first-rate airplane crash...the noise, the flames, the chaos and the suspension of time are beautifully caught." And if you sit right in front of your TV, a couple of feet away, you will have a panic attack, a crying jag, or a transcendental elation. I say this out of experience. The first night I watched the movie by myself: I wept uncontrollably, if sentimentally, at the end. The next night my wife began watching the movie with me but couldn't get beyond the first fifteen minutes when she realized a baby being held in his mother's arms dies in the crash. Despite knowing the movie's end (the more or less Hollywood closure), I cried again. And so I watched the movie a third night—and then a fourth, where I tried not to cry at all, and a fifth, where I tried to cry as hard as possible. By the sixth night, I found a YouTube video of the movie's final sequence. Instead of navigating through the entire movie, I could watch the last six minutes and twenty-eight seconds—twelve times.

It sounds masochistic to watch a depiction of a plane crash over and over—especially because this is no ordinary depiction—it's a recreation. And one might assume that watching this movie would heighten a fear of flying. But I have found the opposite to be true. In Max's near-death experience, you see how calm and at peace he is. Perhaps coming from another actor (Mel Gibson was first asked to play the part), this would appear false or sappy. But Bridges—whose gestures and facial expressions remind me of a cross between my father and an old high school friend—is able to transcend the scene, and dare I say it, the movie itself.

If there's any underlying concept behind the movie's crash scene and climax, it's that fear is the master not just of flying but of all contemporary life. Besides the movie's last sequence, there's another scene that sticks with me. Bridges (I can no longer think of him as Max) is trying to convince a nerve-wracked Rosie Perez to take a drive with him around San Francisco; he says, "I can't explain it, but you're safe with me."

"So what are you telling me," she says, "there's no God—but there's you?"

It's a rhetorical question—*of course he's not God*—but after all the things I've tried to get over my fear on a plane, there are only one or two that help me more than picturing Jeff Bridges in *Fearless*. He might as well be God. And what's God doing in the very last moment of the movie? As hard as he can, he is laughing and crying at the same time.

IT OFFERS SUCH BEAUTIFUL PROMISE: Calm masses of air travelers, reading their *Odysseys*, Bibles, and *Thousand Nights*, with

 CHECKING OUT

Kindles, Sony Readers, Nook E-Readers, iPads, or whatever the next electronic reading invention calls itself.

Around 2006, Sony marketed its e-book "Reader" aggressively in the ambiance of flight: One common magazine ad showed a departure lounge with a sign inviting passengers to read their time away while waiting at their gates. The airport was staged as *the place* to read. By extension, the Sony Reader was offered as *the way* to read: The savvy traveler was promised that he/she could "Fit 80 books in your carry on." Yet wouldn't you go crazy if you actually had the time to read 80 books while sitting at an airport, waiting for a flight that was getting delayed, and delayed, and delayed? Would electronic reading really serve as a solace here? On the other hand, many businesses conduct interviews in airports today; why not college courses? As a literature professor I might enjoy leading a seminar in an airport lounge. The rigid seats would keep students from sleeping, and just being in the airport three times a week for 16 weeks might wear down my trepidation about flying.

As a writer and poet, I have mixed thoughts about electronic readers. If someone is reading a real book you can tell at least partially what they are reading—a novel, a textbook, a romance. If someone is reading a Kindle, you can't tell what they are reading—a novel, an email, a magazine. And that feels like a violation of some kind of rule of reading. And if you are reading a novel, you know exactly how much of the book you have left to read—you think, *Oh, there's only a quarter-inch left, this guy had better wrap up the plot fast!* With a Kindle, you scroll and you have percentages and text locations—but the sensual tactility is gone. That is, you can no longer *feel* what you are reading. I love to be able to hold a book—the paper, the binding, the cover image, the textures of a book can't be replaced by a digital thingamabob. I also like to write comments in the margins or cross out excerpts I don't agree with. This gives the book a kind of biography. I realize that you can add comments in a Kindle, but it's simply not the same. Not the real handwriting, not the real fading of the handwriting over time.

It's like in art—when photography first arrived people thought it would replace painting, but they didn't realize that painting was doing something beyond conveying a picture or an image. Part of a painting's attraction is the paint itself—the texture, gesture, and thickness of materials. And so, too, a book does more than convey information. Or at least it has that possibility. For instance, I have many times slept with books in my bed. I don't see myself doing that with a Kindle: once you've had one Kindle you've had them all.

ALSO BY CHRISTOPHER SCHABERG

The Textual Life of Airports

CHECKING IN
CHRISTOPHER SCHABERG

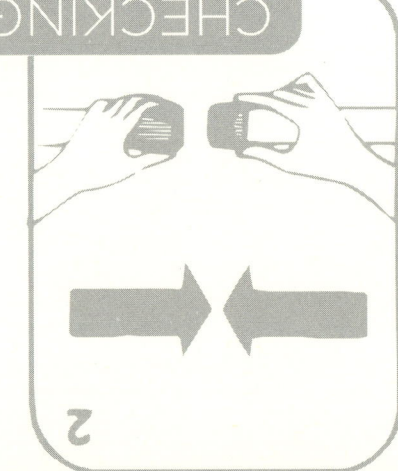

Copyright © 2011 by Christopher Schaberg & Mark Yakich.
All rights reserved.

NO
BOOKS

533 Webster St.
New Orleans, LA 70118

Acknowledgements
For publication of excerpts of this book, thank you to *Brevity*, *The Millions*,
Narrative Magazine, *The New York Times*, and *Propeller Magazine*.

For advice and financial support, thank you to the English Department of
Loyola University, to Mary McCay, and to John Synder of the Center for
Music and Arts Entrepreneurship. This book is sponsored, in part, through
the Center's "The Year of the Writer" initiative.

For design, collaboration, and dear friendship, thank you to Nancy.

For time, inspiration, and love, thank you to Lara and Annie.

ISBN: 978-0-615-46640-8
Design & layout by Nancy Bernardo.
Printed by Thomson-Shore in Dexter, Michigan.

For more airport & airplane stories, visit: airplanereading.org

CHECKING IN

Christopher Schaberg

CROSS-UTILIZED AGENT

A LONG FRONTAGE ROAD RUNS from the town of Bozeman, Montana, to the airport eight miles away in Belgrade. The
Bridger Mountains trail off on the northern horizon—bulging
humps of gray and dark green that rise up off the valley floor.

It was a March morning in 2001, and I was driving out
to the airport—not to fly, but to apply for a job. The newspaper
ad bore the logo of United Airlines, and the position title was
"cross-utilized agent." I parked my old Volkswagen Jetta in the
short-term parking lot, and strolled across the lot to the curb-
side sliding doors.

I have always liked to fly. I feel a weirdly sustained high
when checking in for a flight, waiting to board, and looking at
the ground fall away during takeoff. So the thought of working at an airport was exciting—I would get to see what happens
behind the scenes.

As I entered the controlled environment of the terminal, I spotted the United Airlines sign and walked up to the
counter. There were no passengers in the check-in area; Muzak
floated down from speakers somewhere above. The crisply uniformed agent at the United Airlines desk looked at me skepti-
cally when I asked for a job application; I had a scruffy beard
and a ponytail at the time.

That afternoon, I went to a hole-in-the-wall barber-
shop on Main Street in Bozeman, and had my hair cut short

and neat. I trimmed my beard considerably. When I drove out to the airport the next day to submit my completed application, the same United agent gave me a curt nod of approval as he took my application and turned toward the backroom.

I was called in for a group interview at the airport later that week. The interview took place in a strangely corporate feeling conference room in a nether region of the terminal; I did not realize that airports had rooms that were not dedicated to passengers. In the conference room, I sat around a long table with a dozen or so other applicants, each of us touting our qualifications. It was surprisingly grueling, and at times very embarrassing. Later that day, I got a phone call inviting me for a follow-up interview the next day: this time, it was just the manager Lance, the supervisor Brad, and myself.

Two days later, to my excitement, I was hired to work part-time for SkyWest Airlines, a small regional carrier that flew under the livery of United Express. SkyWest operated two Canadair Regional Jets (CRJ) that flew from Santa Barbara to Denver, and from Denver to Bozeman—and then back, three times a day.

By 2010, SkyWest planes would be servicing 136 cities under the sign of United, and operating over 250 CRJs. During the time I worked for SkyWest, I witnessed the ramping up of this trend toward regional aircraft: a shift from Boeing 737

and Airbus 319/320 (100–150+ passenger airliners) that rarely filled to capacity on short domestic routes, in favor of the 50-seat jets that the airlines could fill up with passengers—and thus, with revenue.

One of the parts of my initial job training—a long week spent in a drab office complex somewhere in downtown Salt Lake City—involved memorizing the hundreds of three-letter airport codes around the country. There was my station, BZN; and then ORD, ATL, DFW, GRR, DTW, MSP, DEN, LGA, MIA, SMF, MSY, JFK, SFO, OAK, LAX, SEA, PDX, TVC, PHX, PSP, SBA.... The list goes on and on, and these codes still pop up in my mind at random intervals—little fragments of geographic identifiers running through my brain. In Salt Lake City (SLC), I watched videos about how to move around planes without scratching the wings or getting decapitated, and I was given a thick three-ring binder full of safety tips and awkward acronyms, airline slogans and corporate ideals.

Yes, my official job title was "cross-utilized agent." This meant that I not only checked in passengers for their flights, and boarded them at the gate; I also handled baggage, de-iced the aircraft when it was freezing, cleaned planes at night, and maintained all the auxiliary vehicles: from the "belt-loader" baggage conveyor to the squat "Tug" tractor used to haul around baggage carts; from the loud external generator to

 CHECKING IN

the silent lavatory reservoir on wheels. I was immersed in all the processes that I had watched take place outside so many window seats. These machines and practices were no longer esoteric or exotic looking—they now comprised my workplace.

CHECKING IN

NOT LONG AGO, CHECKING IN for flights was a social experience. You would go to the airport and line up with other people, some of whom you might see on your flight. Likewise, the airline ticket agents would administer the experience for all, issuing boarding passes and looking into possible upgrades.

With the bloom of online services and the proliferation of automated check-in kiosks at airports, the practice of checking in has become more dispersed and less social. Checking in is now one of those myriad modern practices that invite people to pay to do tasks that used to count as paid labor: the labor of checking in for a flight, selecting seats, and printing boarding passes has been moved away from the paid airline employee at the airport, and is now part of the common traveler's home office experience. Some might celebrate this as putting the power into the hands of the people. Nevertheless, passengers are now doing for free what others used to be trained and paid to do.

When I worked at the airport, there was still the mys-

4

tique of the moody ticket agent. I mastered the comportment of the fickle airline employee, ironically leaning into the counter and propping one foot up on the metal bar that ran about six-inches off the ground across the bottom of the counter. My blue-striped, collared United shirt was pulled taut against my shoulder blades. The mat under my feet was one of those gel-filled cushions made for the type of work that requires long stretches of standing up.

In those days, check-in began exactly two hours before the flight. I learned how to be fiercely oblivious to passengers who were itching to check in before the two-hour mark. I knew how to tilt my head at a certain angle, furrow my brow, and stare deeply into the computer monitor, clicking the keyboard occasionally, while passengers too early to check in stood in line before me trying to make unsubtle sounds in their throats and crinkle their itinerary papers so as to grab my attention.

While standing there, sometimes I used the time to read the United Airlines weekly briefing; there was a quiz to do upon completion, and our scores were sent to our managers. If I had already finished this chore, it was still policy not to begin checking in passengers before two hours—I would find something else to do, like scanning what flights were delayed across the country, and for what reasons.

 CHECKING IN

At two hours before the flight—not a second before—I would look up with a bright smile, and say, "Checking in for the flight to Denver?"

SEATBACK POCKETS

THE AIR HUNG HEAVY ABOVE the taxiway, sweltering hot in the summer, and moist with blue mists of propylene glycol deicing fluid in the winter. And always, that ubiquitous burnt aroma of jet engine exhaust.

Working on the tarmac my hands grew calloused and raw from handling luggage, and the panoramic view consisted of either A) the sliding doors leading out to the short-term parking lot, or B) a dull gray swath of concrete and asphalt leading out to the fenced perimeter of the airfield. The mountain peaks of the Bridger Range seemed to hover far in the background, a disjunctive wilderness that floated above my gritty workspace like in an Ukiyo-e print.

My least favorite job at the airport was cleaning out the seatback pockets every night. After the last arrival, sometime between 10:00 pm and 1:00 am, depending on the weather in Denver, the aircraft spent the night in Bozeman, and part of my job was to thoroughly clean the plane before the end of my shift. The easy part, believe it or not, was the lavatory: it's such a wonderfully small space, and all covered with smooth plastic and

elegant curves. You could spray all the surfaces with a generic and powerfully smelling unnamed cleaner, and wipe down every inch of the space in a few minutes, leaving the mini toilet, mini sink, mini mirror, and mini floor sparkling.

Even dumping the lavatory's actual contents from a slot on the exterior of the plane was efficient and almost fun. I would snap on some big black rubber gloves, hook up a big black tube, unlock the valve, and coax all the solid matter and accompanying "blue juice" into a low-profile reservoir on wheels—the "lav cart." I only splashed shit on myself a few times, and when clumps of fecal matter are bright blue, somehow it all seems okay.

But then, at a certain point, I had to go back inside the plane and face the 50 seatback pockets. The seatback pockets on the new CRJ aircraft at the turn of the century were particularly vexing, because the elastic bands at the top of the pockets were very tight, still fresh from the factory, and this made it awkward to wedge a full hand in, in order to clean out the trash. And you'd never know what the "trash" would consist of.

Good seatback pockets might house a folded magazine, a gum wrapper, or the crumpled stub of a boarding pass. Bad seatback pockets would contain the actual gum, puddles of Pepsi, crushed Crystal Geyser water bottles impossibly wedged in the bottom of the pocket, an exploded pen wrapped in an

CHECKING IN

inky napkin, congealed mini pretzels or cheddar-ranch crackers, gobs of snot caked on indecipherable other matter, or the
razor edge of a boarding pass. Boarding passes could paper-cut
to the bone; I have scars on my knuckles to prove it.

Now, sometimes when I fly my right hand instinctively
makes the precise cupping shape I perfected to swipe out seatback pockets, moving from seat to seat to seat, across the aisle,
back and forth, as so many midnight hours of my life passed by.

Before my airport job, I believed that the wilderness
was a far off place, located somewhere in the mountains or off
in the desert. After working at the airport, I started to think
of air travel itself as a kind of wilderness zone. Like an isolated
butte or a forest with dense undergrowth, seatback pockets became one of the natural features I learned to navigate, and to
maneuver with precision and attention to detail. Each enclo-
sure its own topography, with its own smell and mystery.

MEAL KITS

SKYWEST USED TO GIVE LITTLE meal kits in colorful card-
board boxes to its passengers on the flights from Santa Barbara
to Denver and from Denver to Bozeman.

At the end of each day, we cross-utilized agents would
clean out the extra meal kits and stack them in our office refrigerator—then they were up for grabs. I would sometimes ar-

rive to work very hungry, and wolf down three or four meal kits before starting my shift. The breakfast kits included a firm banana, a bagel, a plastic tub of cream cheese, and a packet of fruit spread. The lunch kits included a ham and cheese croissant sandwich, one pouch of Dijonaise, a small bag of Fritos, and a cellophane-wrapped cookie. I can still conjure the predictable taste of each of these items, their particular flavors enhanced, or maybe muted—I'm not sure which—after having sat in the compressed air of a jet aircraft for a day.

The other staple ration at the airport was the standard airline snack-mix. Here I am referring to those miniature silvery bags that contain indeterminate conglomerates of cheddar-and-ranch dusted crackers, pretzel twists, bagel chips, and/or tortilla triangles. The contents are best consumed in a single open-bag lift to the mouth, and gobbled up in one not-so-enormous bite. After six or seven bags, I was usually full enough to go unload a plane full of luggage, or de-ice the aircraft before takeoff. We had boxes and boxes of these little bags of snack-mix. Even as they changed themes, names, and ingredients over time, they all seemed to come from Solon, Ohio. I often wondered about that factory in Solon, what it would be like to work there. For instance, how many workers sneak mouthfuls of snack-mix while they are making it? Did the snack-mix workers eat the snack-mix on their breaks? Did

CHECKING IN

the snack-mix workers get to take the factory-rejects home for their kids to eat?

A few months into the job, I was flown to Seattle for several weeks to learn the United Airlines computer and ticketing system. The lessons were taught in a windowless basement room in an office park near the SEA-TAC airport. The lessons went on all day: how to check flight schedules, how to assemble an itinerary, how to book a reservation, how to change a reservation, how to cancel a reservation, how to issue flight credits for cancellations due to mechanical problems, and so on. I learned that masterful technique of clicking maniacally away at a keyboard while saying things like "Hmmm...well...I'm sorry, but it doesn't look like there are any available flights to your destination until next Tuesday."

I remember taking the bus into downtown Seattle some afternoons and eating smoked salmon at the Pike Place Market. But aside from a vague memory of an office park cafeteria, and the taste of sour concentrated orange juice, I have little recollection of what else I ate during those long training days in Seattle, those hours spent in the dark basement room, staring at a blue screen, making hypothetical reservations for imaginary people, sending no planes anywhere, not yet, but getting ready to.

Soon after I returned to Bozeman, the meal kits were

discontinued. The last few meal kits in our refrigerator were consumed unceremoniously, the little sprightly boxes crumpled and discarded, gone forever.

TETRIS

I OFTEN THOUGHT OF LOADING baggage as a game of human-scale Tetris. Usually each 50-passenger flight that I worked would require two standard size luggage carts full of roller bags, snowboard carriers, ski bags, Pelican cases, octagonal metal film canisters, long plastic fishing rod cylinders, and hard-sided suitcases. Occasionally there would be a kayak, or a casket.

The tail cargo section of the Canadair Regional Jet is roughly six feet wide by six feet deep by six feet tall at the apex. On any normal day, I would have about 10 minutes in which to load the objects in such a way that A) they all fit, B) nothing was squashed, and C) the load would not cascade dangerously onto the baggage handler upon the flight's arrival.

There are different styles that baggage handlers adopt. These include: 1) Hard-sided suitcases, flat, all across the bottom, and build up from there; 2) Large roller bags lined vertically on their sides along the back wall, followed by duffel bags and then ski and snowboard cases on top; 3) Small roller bags always in the front-most portion, nearest to the cargo door; 4) Don't plan at all: throw it all in and try for a grand, chaotic

CHECKING IN

pyramid that somehow stays intact. The fourth technique is the most common. I learned to always leave room for the inevitable five to 20 carry-on bags that were too big for the mini overhead bins or for under the seats of the CRJ, and therefore had to be crammed in at the last minute, which was like the bonus round of this game of Tetris.

Instead of losing the game when I could not fit a piece in place, usually I just ended up with a badly bruised shin, pinched fingers, crushed toes, or a hard-sided golf case collapsing onto my head as I waited for the next bag to make its way up the belt-loader conveyor.

On any given day, I would go through this routine several times throughout my shift. After a while, loading baggage didn't feel like a game anymore. It felt like work.

NO LONGER NEW

NEW AIRPLANES SMELL LIKE THE future. The CRJs that flew in and out of Bozeman were brand new, and they gave off fresh scents of plastic, metal, and leather. Even the grease around the landing gear had an aromatic quality and an appealing opacity. The lettering on the side of the planes was bold and unmarred, and the aircraft doors opened with a satisfying click-suck-pop sound.

But I recall one day when the aircraft landed in

Bozeman and the wings of the plane were covered with dents and nicks in the paint job. There had been a major hailstorm in Denver, and the CRJ no longer had its fresh-from-the-factory sheen. In my job training we had learned about how critical it was that the flying surfaces of the aircraft were never, ever compromised—but this plane was clearly going to take off again in 25 minutes and make its way to Denver.

At first, it seemed crucial to distinguish a serious risk from standard operating procedure. Once the job was no longer new, though, flight ceased to seem so delicate. Eventually, many of the nose cones of the CRJ aircraft were off color, suggesting quick replacements at some hub, no time to worry about consistent paint jobs. Day in and day out, planes landed and planes took off, and over time everything at the airport became grimy. Gradually, I realized that the futurity of the airport had withered. Flight is really all about the past.

TOM

MY FAVORITE CO-WORKER AT THE airport was Tom. Tom was a big Montana cowboy who managed to at once fulfill and defy every stereotype inherent in that description.

Tom was the hardest worker at the airport: he could handle baggage more efficiently and systematically than anyone else I knew. But he was also playful: he treated the tarmac like a

CHECKING IN

rodeo ring, driving the Tugs around like they were mechanical bucking broncos. Tom also loved to sashay across the tarmac, twirling the heavy black rubber chocks that went around the aircraft landing gear.

Tom had been in the Navy, and had three daughters from a previous marriage. He drove a Ford F-350 SuperCab, and when we'd finish our shift Tom would peel out of the employee parking lot, back tires spitting gravel. Tom could be a show-off, but he was also a good listener. Sometimes when the inbound flight was delayed, we would sit for hours telling each other the stories of our lives, and Tom would always listen intently to my post-college existential musings and life questions.

Tom was a strapping hulk of a guy, and he could be very intimidating to rude passengers: he wouldn't take any guff from passengers jockeying for First Class upgrades, nor would he mince words over a lost bag. Tom was all business.

One time as we were heading out to meet the noon arrival, Tom noticed that I was wearing my SkyWest baseball cap backwards. Tom gave me a lascivious sideways look, and drawled, "There are only two times when I wear a hat like that: when I'm riding my bike, or when I'm sucking somebody off." That was classic Tom, getting in a little moment of fun before hard work, the long plane advancing toward us and the roar of the reverse thrust winding down.

14

Tom manned the jet bridge while I marshaled the aircraft into the gate; Tom gently nudged the beeping bridge up the plane's side, a snug fit. I moved the baggage cart into position and started unloading luggage, while Tom welcomed the deplaning passengers to Bozeman.

All the passengers off the plane and the luggage hurled onto the moving belt of the baggage claim, Tom and I then had to go up to the airport restaurant and get buckets of ice for the next flight. We had to unpack a box of SkyMall catalogs that had just been delivered to United. We had to load the outbound baggage, and finally we had to board the passengers pronto. We only had about 30 minutes to make this all happen and have an on-time departure—our airport's reputation was counting on it. The corporate representative who had stopped by our airport the week before reminded us that we were an important team in the SkyWest family.

Tom was a real worker and a good friend, and working with him made those long days go by quickly. A few years after I left Bozeman, I got an email from Tom inviting me to his wedding—he was marrying another cowboy, with whom he'd built a ranch somewhere in eastern Washington.

Now whenever I see someone wearing a baseball cap backwards, I think of Tom, sucking somebody off. I think of Tom, and I think of all those evenings after the last departure

 CHECKING IN

of the day, each of us in our matching navy blue outfits, United insignias flashing proudly as we raced the Tugs slowly back to the SkyWest garage, into jet exhaust sunsets.

FOD

FOD WAS ONE OF THE corporate acronyms I learned during my job training: it stands for Foreign Objects of Debris. Sometimes, if you look out an airliner window, you may see a nondescript drum on the tarmac with those letters faintly stenciled on it: FOD. This is sort of (but not exactly) like the trashcans at McDonalds or Burger King that say THANK YOU on their flaps.

Whenever there was slack time between flights, we cross-utilized agents were instructed to rove around the tarmac searching for FOD. FOD could include Ziploc baggies (usually just the zip parts would be left), soda can tabs, errant screws, washers, or nuts; but most commonly, FOD consisted of plastic wheels and metallic hubs broken off cheap roller bags heaved in and out of jets. While picking up this certain species of FOD, I often thought of that flashy commercial for a fancy roller bag, how the classy traveler whizzes through the airport to catch his flight, pulling his slick race car roller bag—and then the ad cuts to some poor schlub with an overstuffed duffel bag who bumps into other travelers, trips over things, and eventually hobbles up to a gate that says FLIGHT DEPARTED.

16

Another regularly found type of FOD: zipper pulls—but never ones that read YKK. If you were to get down on your hands and knees on any tarmac and start crawling around, you would find a zipper pull within a few minutes. The narrow end would be severed or shattered where a baggage handler scraped the side of the bag it belonged to against a stronger metal edge. There are probably millions of derelict zipper pulls scattered around airports all over the world, accumulating like an abandoned currency, waiting to be excavated by future archaeologists.

AIRPORT CREATURES

AT FIRST I ONLY SAW airplanes and people: flying machines, and the human passengers that would go in and out of these machines. The longer I worked in this odd environment, however, I started to notice something curious: there were creatures at the airport everywhere I looked.

First there were the inanimate ones: a stylized V of Canada geese sculptures hanging from the terminal ceiling; the big bronze grizzly bear sitting at the base of the escalators; even a sculptural cougar, frozen in flight, leaping out over the baggage claim. These pieces of art were supposed to evoke the Wild West, an idea of animals running free across the frontier...right through the modern airport.

 CHECKING IN

Gradually I began to see more lively creatures abounding at the airport—lively even when sometimes dead. For instance, one June afternoon the United Express CRJ descended smoothly, landed gracefully, and taxied to the gate like any other day. My co-worker marshaled the aircraft in, and when the plane jerked to a stop I crawled under the wing to place the chocks around the landing gear—standard operating procedure. As I scooted under the wing and swung the heavy rubber triangular blocks around the aft wheels of the plane, the smell was familiar yet also peculiar: the usual aroma of aviation fuel exhaust, but mixed with...something else. I suddenly became aware of red splotches dotting the belly of the plane. Then I noticed a quarter-size piece of bone or brain that had been thrown up into the landing gear cavity.

As I squirmed out from under the plane, the captain clambered down the steps and jogged over. He shouted over the Auxiliary Power Unit screaming in the background, "A jackrabbit hopped out onto the runway just as we landed! We clipped him good! Woo wee! Look at all that blood!" There were little chunks of flesh and fur dangling from the wing flaps.

Meanwhile, the passengers deplaned, utterly oblivious to the minor scene of horror behind them. My co-worker and I unloaded the baggage, boarded the outbound passengers, and turned the plane around in the obligatory 30 minutes.

18

The pulverized remains of the jackrabbit flew to Denver, and onward. This gave new meaning to the term "sky burial," which before this I had understood only in a Tibetan Buddhist context.

Then there was the morning of the great Delta gopher snake. The 737 had over-nighted on the tarmac one fall evening, and the next morning a huge gopher snake was discovered curled around the nose landing gear. Apparently the snake had crawled up into the landing gear cavity in Salt Lake City (or somewhere prior), and then slithered down onto asphalt in Bozeman.

It occurred to me that this sort of counted as an evolved form of migration: the snake had found a rather quick way to a new bioregion. And then it dawned on me that, strictly speaking, evolution encompasses everything that happens; there's no getting outside of it. Airports are a human phenotype, and other creatures interpenetrate these techno-cultural spaces, showing them to be actual ecosystems, through and through. And years later, when I saw a poster for the movie *Snakes on a Plane*, I didn't think it sounded creepy or tantalizing—it seemed entirely plausible.

One time I walked out of the back room of the United baggage bay and noticed a mound of what looked like excrement clinging to the wall. On closer inspection, it was a bat

CHECKING IN

that had hunkered down to wait out the day on the cool, shaded north face of the terminal. When I got closer, I saw how beautiful it was: slightly furry, more blue-gray than black, its tiny eyes watching me watch it.

But I could not tarry in this naturalist state of observation; there was a pile of luggage to load onto the plane. After loading the baggage, as I drove the Tug back across the tarmac, I watched from afar as one of my co-workers saw the bat and promptly crushed it with the end of a hard-sided golf club case.

I think antagonism toward other flying creatures is often heightened around airports, and not just because of the threat of airborne collisions. Other flying creatures also pique repressed fears that humans have overextended their reach in the world—a nagging worry that perhaps we shouldn't be flying at all. But again: if this is our phenotype, there will be no easy way to undo it.

Late one night I was in the middle of cleaning the inside of the aircraft, near the end of my shift. I was wiping a child's magic marker scribbles off the retractable window shade when I noticed a translucent, still insect lying between the plastic interior screen and the external pressurized glass pane. It was suspended in this space, its miniature wings extended so that I could see the points of articulation and its delicate yet refined flying surfaces. I was reminded of Virginia Woolf's essay "The

Death of a Moth," which focuses intensely on a dying moth, and concludes that death is stronger than us all. As I looked at the small bug, I wondered at what point had it become incarcerated between the plane's windowpanes. Did the moth get in the window recess in the factory, during the plane's construction? Or had this bug, in Santa Barbara or Denver, exploited a weak seam or gap in the plane's allegedly airtight construction? For how long had this plane always been a mobile sarcophagus of sorts?

Sometimes as planes would taxi to the gates the pilots would radio in and request a "bug wipe." This meant that on descent they'd collided with a cloud of insects, and the smeared corpses would be coating the aircraft's cockpit windows, a hoary tapenade. There was a special ladder that I would carefully wheel up to the nose of the plane, and I'd climb up the ladder carrying a window wiper that was like those found at gas stations between pumps. I'd spray some generic cleaning fluid on the angled windows, and swipe and rub, swipe and rub, until all the bugs were gone, their minuscule bodies floating in a bucket of grayish blue, destined for the industrial drain on the tarmac. Bird strikes are a popular subject, raising questions of everyday danger and ecological significance. Bug strikes, on the other hand, are all but ignored, at once too small, vastly outnumbering, and myriad for most people to care about. But how many things do humans tune out, simply as a matter of scale?

Airport creatures tuned me in to some environmental aspects of human flight, to a sort of zoomed out view of how we travel and how we come into contact with other beings across scales of time and significance. These experiences have caused me to wonder how air travel distances us from the reality of living with others, even as it also brings us closer together.

BURNOUT

I UNDERSTAND WHY SOME PEOPLE are terrified of flying. It's true that any ordinary flight might turn into a spectacular disaster.

One time during a lazy evening shift I heard some commotion next door at the Delta counter. I peeked around the wall and saw the Delta crew huddled around their station manager. The Delta manager was talking in a hushed but urgent tone about their inbound flight. I pretended to be picking up rubbish off the terminal carpet, and listened.

Apparently one of the plane's engines had a burnout in mid-flight, and it might turn into an emergency landing if the other engine went. The plane was eight miles out. The airport fire trucks had been called and were rushing to the end of the runway, anti-fire foam at the ready. The faces of the Delta workers reflected a mixture of excitement, panic, and sudden bewilderment: cross-utilized agents were not trained to handle runway skids.

I raced around the check-in counter and through the supply room, out the United door, and watched as the Delta Connection CRJ descended between the Bridger peaks and the north end of the Gallatin range. The landing lights winked on. The plane glided in elegantly, and landed like all the others I had seen before, except for the three chartreuse fire trucks, lights flashing, raced behind the plane—I remember thinking that the fire trucks' engines were louder than the plane's reverse thrust.

I was oddly disappointed. No crash landing, no harrowing escape by passengers jumping onto emergency chutes, no one calling on me to lend a hand, United and Delta workers joined in camaraderie. It was just another plane to be unloaded, cleaned, inspected, repaired...and sent off again into the blue.

I think I remember that the tail of the plane was scorched behind the engine that had burned out in flight. But I might have exaggerated or even invented the vision in my mind, mixed as it is with various movie scenes, headlines, and news photos of planes sitting at the end of the runway or off in a ditch, after an emergency landing or a botched takeoff.

FLIGHT PRIVILEGES

AS AN AIRLINE EMPLOYEE I could fly for free, practically anywhere. Of course, flying for free not only meant flying

CHECKING IN

stand-by: it also meant flying stand-by with lowest possible priority, below paying passengers trying to get on earlier flights, below pilots and other crew members, and below all the mainline airline employees. This made travel hard to plan, but this also made it exciting. I used my flight privileges as often as I could. I flew around the country to see friends and family, and sometimes just to Denver and back on a whim. There was something alluring about striking out for the airport and *not* knowing if I would be able to fly or not.

At the Gallatin Field Airport we enjoyed what was called a "station agreement" between airlines: any airline employee could fly stand-by (or "non-revenue" in the parlance) on any of the airlines. So, as a SkyWest United Express worker, I could fly stand-by not only on United flights, but also on Delta, Northwest, and Horizon (regional carrier for Alaska Airlines). These flight privileges were a major perk for an airline employee. And yet, most of the people I worked with at the Gallatin Field Airport rarely used their flight privileges: they had families, second jobs, or worked full-time, and therefore could not get away so easily.

You needed to be pretty flexible to fly stand-by as an airline employee: you'd take off for Denver, Salt Lake City, Minneapolis, or Seattle, and unless that was your endpoint, you'd likely have to make any number of uncertain connec-

24

tions in order to make it to your "final destination"—you might end up flying four different airlines, zigzagging all across the country, just to make it to San Francisco and back over a two-day break. Usually you'd return exhausted, and just in time for work. But if you had an adventurous spirit, it was a blast—it could be as wild as running rapids on the Snake River. Flying stand-by regularly also made the work more exciting, because a sense of personal suspense started to pulsate through the entire network of flight: the whole operation seemed held together by thin threads of time and tenuously maintained spaces.

And yet the reality was that for most people who worked at the airport, it was just that: *work*. It was not a chance to travel for free (or if so, *very* rarely), and neither was it a unique or interesting job. The starting pay was around seven dollars an hour, and the hours were often miserable. The work was tedious, repetitive, and physically taxing: hefting several tons of awkward-sized luggage every day; standing in front of a computer screen checking in passengers and occasionally being castigated for incompetence over a weather delay somewhere across the country; transporting crates of soda cans out to the planes...these things quickly chipped away at the romance of flight. Further-more, the chances for promotion were rather slim. I did see my operations manager, Lance, become the regional manager in Denver; and the supervisor Brad moved up to the new op-

CHECKING IN

erations manager in Bozeman and then eventually went on to become the operations manager in Salt Lake City. So there was a kind of professional mobility, but rather than purely upward, it was more outward, angular, and dispersed.

If I Google my old co-workers today, I can find traces of their lives, like little lines of flight: snapshots of happy families in the snow, or stylized Facebook profile pictures with familiar grins or serious looks, their hands holding beers or kids, sometimes making unclear gestures, maybe faux gang signs. For a time we all worked together at a small airport in Montana. The airline we worked for told us we were a "team"— but I wasn't sure who we were competing against, or when the game was supposed to end. On the other hand, what we were doing *did* have high risks, whether that meant breaking the aircraft, or finding oneself stranded in a remote airport amid a stand-by spree around the country, while trying to get back to work.

STRANDED

ONE EARLY SPRING DAY I used my flight privileges to hop over to Michigan to visit my parents. Because the flights were relatively empty, I flew First Class on Northwest both legs, Bozeman to Minneapolis, Minneapolis to Traverse City. It was the perfect stand-by excursion. I enjoyed an omelet on the first flight, and a generous glass of syrah as the second flight cruised

26

past the Wisconsin shoreline and I looked down at the Manitou Islands in Lake Michigan.

A couple days later I had to fly back to Bozeman to work the next morning. I left plenty early, to give myself a full 24 hours to get home. The first flight went smoothly, Traverse City to Detroit, a 50-minute hop across a state of decay. But I was excited to see the new Detroit airport, with its red bullet tram that whooshed above the concourse, connecting the farthest gates in a matter of minutes.

In Detroit I was waiting to catch a connecting flight to Salt Lake City when a classic Midwestern storm grayed out the sky, dumped heavy wet snow, and abruptly shut down the airport. I didn't have a credit card at that time in my life, and had only about 15 dollars in my wallet.

So that night I slept on the floor of the brand new McNamara World Gateway concourse. I was no longer a giddy First Class flier, but rather was relegated to the wretched status of a postmodern nomad. As I rolled out my highly compressible sleeping bag on the floor, I experienced the weird thrill of urban wilderness. The carpet, however, still smelled new, and had a certain firm softness to it. The fluorescent lights glowed through my closed eyelids, making for phantasmagoric dreams. Lulled by distant announcements for people to pick up the white courtesy phone, I fell into a deep sleep.

I opened my eyes at some point in the nether hours long past midnight, awakened by a strange sensation of synchronized motion and sound. I raised my head slightly and looked around, while trying not to draw attention to my humble bivouac.

About 50 feet down the concourse was a cleaning crew, working in total unison, their outfits as crisp and conforming as the new airport concourse that they were cleaning. Their vacuums and litter-plucking devices looked futuristic, and they roved expertly in and out of the departure gates, cleaning every seat surface, picking up every discarded boarding pass and Starbucks cup, and dropping them into sleek rolling and pivoting trashcans. They cleaned right around my sleeping bag, treating my prone body as another feature of the concourse—or more likely, having been trained not to disturb the passengers.

Little did they know that I was a mere worker, too, waiting out the night, hoping to catch a morning flight in order to get back in time for my shift. As I drifted back to sleep, I tabulated my chances of making it back to Bozeman on time, mentally mapping the routes my flight privileges could take to deposit me back at my airport, back to work.

STRANGE FLIGHTS

I HAD MOVED TO BOZEMAN for a Master's program in Eng-

lish. My airport job paid the rent all spring and summer, as I covered many of my co-workers' shifts; within a few months I could practically run the airport by myself. I remember the startled look on passengers' faces when they'd see me boarding them at the upstairs departure gate after having just checked them in for their flight downstairs a half hour ago; and then they'd see me outside a few minutes later loading their baggage onto the plane, before finally hopping onto the diesel push-back Tug and sending them down the taxiway.

Starting in the fall of 2001, my other part-time job commenced: teaching freshman composition three mornings a week as part of my graduate work. This involved reading the essays of dutiful ranchers' children and transplant trustafarians alike, with the former group having a more intuitive knack for descriptive prose.

September 11 was my day off. On my days off, when I was fly-fishing or hiking, I would find myself subconsciously tracking inbound flights and takeoffs, distant jet blasts and glints of silver in the sun. I remember the absence of planes that day as a kind of kink in the muscle memory that any job creates over time: where Delta's 737 usually flew overhead from Salt Lake City at noon, there was only silence and sky.

I was scheduled to work at the airport the following afternoon, on September 12. But first I had a class to teach. It

CHECKING IN

was my first time teaching at the college level, and we were only a few weeks into the semester; I was 23 years old. I recall sitting in a discussion circle with 30 freshmen on that day, not really knowing what to say.

As I tried to direct attention to our course anthology, I remember one student who was so upset that he blurted out in class, "We need to bomb people, NOW!"

When I tried, in my most affected professorial tone, to gingerly ask the class to consider the construction of the "we" in this claim, and whom exactly it was "we" should bomb, the same student screamed back at me, "*ANYBODY!*" His idea seemed to be that by inflicting firepower by air on other people, the United States could steal the show: the products of our military jets would be the focus of attention, and take away from the spectacle of four commercial airliners having gone rogue.

And a spectacle it was. When I walked over to the student union after class for lunch, I saw that several large TV screens had been wheeled into the open spaces between the seating areas. Some students filtered in and out of the dining hall like normal, scooping out helpings of macaroni and cheese; other students stood transfixed, watching reruns of the planes crashing again and again and again into the towers of the World Trade Center. The event was being familiarly looped, and the

ambience of the instant replay created a warm, somewhat stale sensation—despite the chillingly fresh content.

That afternoon, I drove out to the airport for my shift. I had tried to call in to figure out if flights were on time, or if I even had to work—but the lines were all busy. I decided to play it safe and just show up. When I got to the airport, the scene was one of stunted pandemonium. The terminal seemed at once totally chaotic and oddly frozen. Yes, my manager explained, I was still needed for work; but there were no flights due in or out that day. However, they could start back up at any moment—so we had to be ready.

In the meantime, there was a line of skittish passengers to deal with, people who were scheduled on flights that were not going to depart. These passengers didn't realize, perhaps, the scope of what had occurred the day before, how all the commercial airlines had simply been grounded into the unforeseeable future. Not that we airline employees knew any better: the best we could do was reschedule the passengers on flights a day or a week later, send them off with newly printed itineraries, and cross our fingers.

After assisting a dozen or so confused and distraught passengers who were feeling the logistical back-blow of what would come to be called 9/11, I went back into the break room and saw my manager Lance taping onto the wall a few photo-

CHECKING IN

graphs of himself directing a C-130 Air Force cargo plane onto our taxiway. This was one of the strange flights that had landed at our airport the day before; Lance had taken the roll of film to a one-hour photo lab that evening and had them printed out, and now was displaying them like little trophies. Lance told me excitedly that a Stealth bomber had landed in Bozeman, too; but it had refueled and taken off again before anyone could get a picture of it.

The next day, I rummaged through the files on my desk, and found an essay that appeared in the Spring 2001 Patagonia outdoor clothing catalog. This short piece was called "Homage to Faizabad," and it was written by the journalist Rob Schultheis; he was covering a drawn-out war in Afghanistan. The essay begins beautifully:

> We've been flying for nearly an hour,
> with nothing below us but the raw gorges
> and snow-covered peaks of the Hindu
> Kush. Somewhere down there are villages,
> fields, roads and trails, and the war we have
> returned to cover, but it's all lost in dis-
> tance, space and scale in the vastness that
> is Afghanistan.

Schultheis goes on to describe the isolated town of Faizabad, including the friendly people he meets amid the wheat

32

fields, pastures, and poppy fields. I took this essay to campus the following day and photocopied it for my students; in class, we took turns reading it aloud, slowly, paragraph by paragraph. We talked about the expository strategies that the author employed, including the initial focalizing mechanism of an aerial view; we also talked about the real people depicted in the essay, people caught up a long history of conflicts and power struggles in this place freshly glossed in the news, Afghanistan.

Over the next several days I kept arriving at the airport to work only to face passengers who felt immobilized, and who were becoming increasingly frustrated that air travel had not started up again. As airline employees, we were not trained to explain the conditions and contingencies of a national state of emergency—instead, we would concentrate in front of our computer monitors, fingers clicking away, and rebook the passengers on theoretical future flights, exuding less confidence by the day in the following day's departures. Still, it was our job, and so we carefully rescheduled passengers using a booking system that increasingly felt like dabbling in postmodern fiction: we were creating complex itineraries that would never be.

Some passengers came back to the airport day after day trying to fly out of Bozeman. Their travel clothes became rumpled looking, and they had less confidence on their faces every time they came through the sliding doors of the termi-

CHECKING IN

nal. It became more of a travesty with each day: people showing up with full suitcases and long faces, only to trudge back to
the long-term parking lot a couple minutes later, after we had
turned them away. Yet sure enough, one day a full plane flew in
from Denver, and air travel was back on.

By the end of the semester I was teaching my students
about narrative perspective, and we were discussing how things
could be examined from multiple angles. My students read Mark
Twain's "Two Views of the Mississippi," and we parsed his two
takes on the riparian landscape: that of the Romantic river gazer,
and that of the jaded riverboat worker. Now, it seemed as though
there was a third perspective we needed to talk about, one that we
had encountered in Schultheis's essay: the view from above. For
at this point the news was flooded with aerial reconnaissance
images of Afghanistan, including the Tora Bora region that
looked not so unlike our own Tobacco Root Mountains
stretched across the western horizon. There were contrails over
those peaks; and on the news we could see weirdly congruous
imagery of peaks on the other side of the planet, rendered by
other planes with different intentions.

Like Twain's philosophical quandary about getting to
know the river, and thus losing a sense of its innate beauty, our
own romance with flight had become complicated. For myself,
I could no longer treat the Gallatin Field Airport as a simple

34

workspace; I saw it enmeshed in politics and power, territory and populations. This was no mere "regional" airport—it was part of a fraught global matrix where all flights were strange flights, and travel was never an isolated endeavor.

CODE RED

I WORKED WITH A WOMAN named Vicki. At first Vicki was suspicious of me because I was a part-timer and a "college guy." But as I picked up more and more shifts for other workers, and proved myself to be a hard worker and a fast learner, she began to soften.

After about six months of Vicki scowling at me throughout our shifts together, one morning she signaled for me to follow her back into the garage where all the baggage carts were parked between flights. I didn't know what we were going to do back there, but I followed her anyway. Next to the baggage carts was our station refrigerator, where we stored all the extra sodas and bottled waters for the aircraft. Without a word, Vicki opened the freezer and pointed inside. Nestled in a small heap of ice were two half-frozen Big Gulps of Mountain Dew Code Red: one for her and one for me. The frosty treat was delicious, and the high-octane caffeine made the next work activities race by.

After that day, whenever we worked together Vicki

35

would buy me a Code Red, and we would go through the same ritual of discovering it in the freezer and then being excited about the cold slushy soda. We would drink them, and then go out to load bags or check the oil level on the Tugs and other vehicles. "Code Red" coincidentally sounded like the terrorist threat level at that time.

Vicki had an impressive mop of orange hair and two children of indeterminate age and equally voluminous bright hair. Sometimes at the end of our shift the kids would be waiting out in the employee parking lot with her husband in a rusted-out tan Jeep, and when Vicki and I would walk out of the unmarked side door of the terminal, the kids would be leaning into the jetwash of the Northwest Airbus 320s that arrived around that time. The kids got as close as they could to the chain link fence, trying not to get knocked down, hair whirling around and flaring up like little forest fires. When I said one day that her kids were cute, she looked at me like I was insane, and told me they were "on-ree."

One morning Vicki and I were working the seven o'clock flight together. We had boarded the passengers and loaded the bags, and were all ready to push back the plane from the gate to taxi to the runway. Vicki was operating the jet-bridge, and I was on the tarmac making sure everything was clear behind the aircraft—that is what "wing walkers" do, those often bored

looking workers who you see holding plastic orange wands erect, standing near the tips of the wings while the plane moves back from the gate.

As Vicki reversed the jet-bridge, pulling away from the CRJ, something caught on the gate, and there was a sharp *pop*. A cotter pin had snapped: the retractable stairs on the plane's front door slammed down, suddenly limp. We stared at the 20 million dollar plane sitting there in the rising sun.

The jet-bridge had snagged a tiny piece of the aircraft door. There was no serious damage to the flying surfaces of the aircraft, but corporate protocol required that we deplane all 50 passengers and reschedule them on different flights. One minute the aircraft had been ready for takeoff; the next minute we had a line of people holding useless boarding passes, and a plane that was going nowhere. Vicki was taken by Lance to the local hospital for a mandatory drug test, another official protocol following any "incident." Short-staffed, the rest of us unloaded the baggage compartment of the plane and rerouted all the passengers on flights later that day. The pilots eventually "dead headed" the empty plane to Salt Lake City for repairs. It was a long morning, but by evening everything was back on schedule.

I never saw Vicki again. I heard a rumor that the drug test had come back positive for cocaine—but I heard lots of ru-

37

 CHECKING IN

mors at the airport, particularly after 9/11. I also heard that Vicki went back to work at Wal-Mart, where she had worked before the airport job opened up.

Ralph Waldo Emerson once wrote an essay called "Circles" that begins: "The eye is the first circle; the horizon which it forms is the second; and throughout nature this primary figure is repeated without end." I'm not sure that Vicki's circular path from Wal-Mart to the airport and back to Wal-Mart was quite what Emerson had in mind—then again, the term "holding pattern" hadn't been invented yet, either. Somehow, circling planes make the geometry of the "primary figure" seem a little less spiritual.

Later that year, Mountain Dew came out with an orange soda called "Live Wire," but I never tried it.

STICKERS

SOON AFTER 9/11, A CASE of stickers arrived at the airport: this was the latest in a series of attempts to outsmart the terrorists.

The red stickers read SECURE, and we were instructed to place a sticker over each door seam on the aircraft whenever the plane was left unattended—whether this was in the daytime during a crew change, or overnight when the airport was all but abandoned. The idea was that if the plane had been accessed

38

while left unattended, we would know: the stickers had a one-time-use seal that if tampered with was easily evident.

Imagine this for a moment. Each day, the plane might be left unattended two or three times. Each time, the red stickers had to be deployed and then torn off when the plane was attended again. Within weeks, the door frames of the aircraft resembled weird palimpsests, tacky material outlining the word SECURE at a hundred different angles. We all shared a tacit understanding that we would continue to use the stickers, even though there would have been no possible way to determine if a sticker had been removed—there were so many bits and pieces of SECURE stickers stuck to the door frames, a desperate demand for security in childish form and scattered indecipherably all over the planes.

Then one day, word came that we no longer had to use the stickers. The remaining rolls of stickers sat in a box in the corner of our office, secure at last.

JEFF BRIDGES

I REMEMBER THE COTTONWOOD LEAVES were turning yellow when I saw it: the name Jeff Bridges on the passenger list printed out in the morning prior to our flights. Jeff Bridges and his three daughters would be checking in for a flight to Santa Barbara. We speculated that they had been spending some time at their home outside of Livingston, and were headed back

CHECKING IN

to California for some interesting reason. Maybe it was the end of summer, and the girls had to be back in school. Or maybe it was for a movie. Either way, we started to recite lines from *The Big Lebowski* in anticipation of Jeff Bridges' arrival.

Our station manager Lance was very excited that Jeff Bridges would be checking in for our flight, and so he had positioned himself steadfastly at the United counter in order to assist the famous actor when he arrived at the airport.

As luck would have it, Lance had to step away to a phone call in his office at the precise moment that the Bridges pulled up to the curb in an old, beat-up Suburban. It was either dark gray or dust-coated black. I stood there looking earnestly into my computer screen, pretending to be busy. I shuffled blank ticket stock and carefully arranged the pens and stapler in a slot above the computer terminal. Jeff Bridges stepped out of the driver's seat and unloaded a surprisingly small number of bags from the rear of the Suburban. His daughters got out of the truck and stood in the glaring sunlight. They left the truck sitting there at the curb and approached the terminal, Jeff Bridges carrying a banjo or something slung over his shoulder, in a case. Then they walked through the sliding doors.

When he walked up to the United counter, I told Jeff Bridges that I liked his performance as "The Dude." He thanked me and said, "Yeah, that was a pretty good show."

40

After looking carefully at Jeff Bridges' ID to make sure he was himself, and the daughters' IDs, too, I printed their boarding passes. It seemed slightly ridiculous, but I asked for and inspected all their IDs, because that is what I was trained to do—I was keeping the country safe. Their seating assignments were all in economy class; they were flying the entire way on our SkyWest CRJ aircraft, which at that point did not have First Class sections. I carefully explained their itinerary to them, making appropriate but not creepy eye contact, and I diagrammed how to get to the right gate in Denver in order to catch their connecting flight. Then I sent them on their way to the second level where the departure lounge was located. And this was curious: they left the Suburban sitting at the curb. I never found out what happened to it, whether it was supposed to be picked up by a friend, or whether it was towed and scrapped.

Jeff Bridges and his daughters waited for their flight to board like everyone else. Then the flight was delayed; and then it was canceled. It must have been a mechanical problem, because I remember re-booking a long line of passengers, sending them to Salt Lake City on Delta, or to Minneapolis on Northwest, or to Seattle on Horizon...instead of to Denver on United.

In the end, Lance got his chance to meet Jeff Bridges. When the passengers had all lined up back at the ticket coun-

CHECKING IN

ter again, Lance strolled out from his office and intercepted Jeff Bridges, who was waiting in line with everyone else; Lance ushered him and his daughters into the backroom, where the daughters lounged on our swivel chairs while Lance personally re-booked them on another flight. I was both impressed and a little put off: Why shelter these people and treat them like royalty, when they were clearly comfortable standing in line with the rest of the disgruntled passengers?

Airports have a peculiar way of reinforcing accepted social norms; it was as if my manager Lance had an obligation to shield the famous actor from the common folk. But this is me looking back at it now ten years on, reflecting on class systems, the society of the spectacle, and celebrity status. At that time, I was too busy re-booking other passengers to think about this kind of thing for very long. In any case, soon Jeff Bridges and his daughters were long gone, and we had another flight to deal with.

A NIGHT ON THE TARMAC

WHEN I STARTED WORKING AT the airport, the job was exciting: crawling under CRJs to place chocks around the landing gear was a real thrill the first few times. Then, most of the job became routine: it was work, and I found myself counting down the hours and then minutes until my shifts were over.

The nightshifts, however, were different. They were a relatively relaxed affair. Here's what happened on any given night: The first hour involved waiting around the check-in counter and answering people's questions about if the flight was on-time—and if not, why not. Only two of us would be working, and once the flight radioed in that it was 15-minutes from landing, we had to prepare the jet-bridge for the flight's arrival. Sometimes we would prepare things well ahead of time; other times, we would wait until the last minute and then rush around like maniacs getting everything ready for the aircraft. It depended what TV movie was playing in our office.

When the plane touched down, we had to marshal it to the gate, deplane the passengers, unload the baggage from the aircraft, dump the baggage at the baggage carousel, rush back to the check-in counter to file missing baggage reports, and finally, after the passengers had gone and the day's paperwork was all complete, we had to clean the plane.

Usually, one of us would return to the counter to take missing bag complaints and file the paperwork. The other one of us would head out to the plane and start cleaning. The first thing to do was to clean the inside of the lavatory. This involved spraying and scrubbing the surfaces of the sink and toilet seat, and replenishing the hand soap, paper towels, and toilet paper roll. Sometimes I would have to use the toilet myself before

CHECKING IN

cleaning it, and this always felt a little strange: sitting on the miniature toilet in an otherwise empty airplane parked for the night under dim lights. I was always nervous that my co-worker would come bounding back onto the plane to help clean while I'd be sitting on the toilet—but it never happened. Still, I was paranoid, and so I would keep the plastic door cracked, and watch through the oval window opposite the lavatory to make sure my co-worker wasn't speeding across the tarmac in a Tug, back to the plane.

When my co-worker would be back on the plane with me, we had to attend to the seat-back pockets, clean the galley, restock drinks, SkyMall catalogs, and emergency briefing cards. The last thing to do was to vacuum the plane. This is trickier than it sounds: our standard-size vacuum would be plugged into an extension cord from the jet-bridge, and the cord had to be uncoiled, recoiled, and guided carefully as I moved through the plane, otherwise the cord could get hung up on the arm-rests, or get tangled around my ankles sending me sprawling into the aisle or across the seats. The easier job was using the handheld vacuum, going over all the seat surfaces—but for neurotic workers like myself, this could turn into a seriously tedious task.

One time I slept overnight on the tarmac, in a bag-gage cart. I had worked the nightshift, which ended at around

1:00 AM, and I had to be at the airport again in the morning at 6:00. Why drive 20 minutes home for a mere four hours of sleep? This seemed ludicrous. So instead, I had put my sleeping bag and my camping mattress in my work locker, and after feigning an exit to my co-worker at the end of the night, I looped back inside the airport, went around the back of the check-in counter and out onto the tarmac by the plane, where I crawled up into the second level of a baggage cart.

In the upper compartment of the baggage cart, I laid out my camping mattress and unpacked my sleeping bag, spreading it out carefully. I took off my uniform and climbed inside my sleeping bag, shivering in the cold mountain air. I listened. It was quiet, the planes all tucked into their gates for the night. I pulled the vinyl curtain closed, and fell asleep. When I woke up it was just before dawn, and the mountains were beginning to turn pink. So was the plane next to me. I rolled out of my sleeping bag, pulled on my rumpled airline shirt and navy blue utility pants, hopped out of the baggage cart, and went to work.

Ever since working at the airport, I always take care to clean up around me when I fly. I never put chewed gum in the seat-back pockets, and I wipe up after myself when I use the lavatory. I make sure to give the flight attendants all of my refuse, and I don't spill snack-mix on my seat, where it might

CHECKING IN

get wedged into little crevasses that someone will have to work extra hard to clean out at the end of the day. I also appreciate the views from the taxiway, even when they appear drab, the horizons smudges of gray. I remember that view from the tarmac at sunrise, when the runways were awash with bubblegum light, and the airplanes started to glow.

EPILOGUE

AFTER FINISHING MY M.A. DEGREE at Montana State University-Bozeman, I moved to Davis, California, where I started a Ph.D. program in English. I started to notice odd airport appearances in all sorts of literary and cultural texts, and I ended up writing my doctoral dissertation about airports in American culture.

In January 2009 I flew to New Orleans, where I was interviewing for a position teaching contemporary literature at Loyola University. The poet Mark Yakich picked me up at the airport, and he took me to lunch at a Lebanese restaurant.

Mark and I started talking about airport scenes in movies and books, and Mark mentioned how he'd recently finished writing a novel that took place, in part, on a plane and in an airport. He proceeded to rattle off some impressive factoids about historic plane crashes.

I had just flown through Denver, where I saw the

wreckage of Continental flight 1404, which a few weeks before had slid off the runway upon takeoff, bursting into flames and ending in a heap alongside the runway, burning brightly in the night. Fortunately everyone on the plane survived, all the passengers escaping as the overhead bins melted over their heads. One passenger, upon exiting the plane, turned and snapped a picture of the plane with his camera phone, and posted it to his Twitter account. As my flight taxied to the gate in Denver, I saw the Boeing 737 cracked in half and sitting lopsided behind a hanger where it had been towed.

I described all of this in detail to Mark, and pulled out my phone to show him a photo I'd seen online of the plane's cabin after the crash.

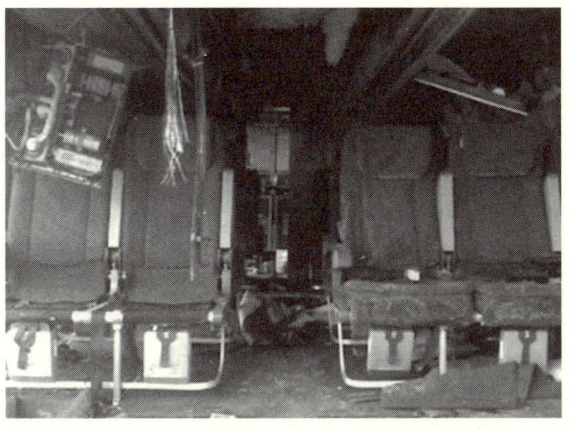

CHECKING IN

I pointed out how you could see which parts of the ceiling had come undone, and how the armrests in their "up" position suggested some very precise commands issued by the flight attendants as the plane skidded to its resting place. When I looked up at Mark I noticed that he had stopped eating; he was holding his lamb kebob midway between his plate and his mouth, and appeared to be on the verge of crying or vomiting—I couldn't discern which—and then he began to tell me about his fear of flying.

 CHECKING OUT

in mind only—until I reach the period. What is it like to read this way? This eye-and-mind act turns into a game like those I played between myself and fate as a kid—*If I make the next five free-throws in a row, Mary Ann will go out with me.* And this is where my hyper-irrationality comes in: I feel that nothing bad will happen in-flight while I am reading mid-sentence, and yet I don't like to prolong mid-sentence for fear that I won't get to the end if something bad does happen. The thought is paradoxical and preposterous, but that doesn't change the fact that the act of reading feels powerful to me. At times such reading feels like a diversion from flying, at other times it feels like an animation of the experience. Once in a while it feels like a bit of both—like that threshold between being asleep and being awake, where for a moment I lose all sense of where and even who I am. Reading in flight: this is checking out at its most sublime, and it allows for an equanimity I simply can't achieve on the ground.

Despite trying a range of remedies, including therapy, meditation, medication, sublimation, and a fear of flying course, I realize I may never be permanently cured of my anxiety. By now, however, I have learned that above all else it is reading itself that helps the most. I don't mean reading the home-remedy escapism of a mystery, romance, or thriller. That doesn't work for me, not because I might not enjoy such books, but because I don't want my potential last thoughts to be the stuff of typical airport reading—throwaway or cheap.

Like flying itself, reading connects me to others through space and time. Particularly on take-off, reading helps because it's the one thing about the flight that feels in my control. It's not that I can start and stop whenever I want; I can do that reading anywhere. It's that on a plane there's absolutely nothing else to do that seems worthwhile besides reading. I can listen to music or watch TV, but those things are passive, and I don't always want to feel so checked out on a plane. Or rather, I want to feel checked out in the right way: Reading is active, and *interactive*—a far greater distraction—for when I do it right, it can become a kind of dialogue between me and whatever I'm reading.

I deliberately begin each sentence as slowly as possible and then with increasing speed I'll read and read—breathlessly

 CHECKING OUT

NOW I FIND MYSELF AGAIN mid-flight, about to open a small book called *Checking In*. My wife, son, and newborn daughter are all here too. We're headed to Chicagoland so that my parents, sister, brother-in-law, and nieces can meet the baby for the first time. My wife is nursing the baby, and my son doesn't want to hold my hand anymore because he says it's "calmy." He means "clammy" but I've taught him the spoonerism because I'm still embarrassed when fellow passengers know about my anxiety.

I know that the plane will continue to hum along punctuated every so often by turbulence. Instead of clutching the armrests, I will wedge the tops of my shoes underneath the supports of the seat in front of me—this will attract less attention from others. I will remind myself that a plane nearly never goes down mid-flight, but then I will recall that some years ago part of the fuselage of a Korean airliner suddenly ripped off at 35,000 feet and eight passengers were sucked into the engine. I will take a deep breath and re-focus on what my senses tell me—that the seat is onerous, but that I am warm and safe inside this aluminum shell, and that it is a fine day out there for flying. The clouds will be especially stunning, quilted across a slate blue sky, and everything will smell as it should—a mix of fresh black coffee, almond-scented hand soap, and artificial rose disinfectant.